GUIDE TO PERSONAL FINANCE

VIRGINIA B. MORRIS

KENNETH M. MORRIS

LIGHTBULB PRESS
Project Team

Design Director Kara W. Wilson
Editor Mavis Wright
Production Thomas F. Trojan

www.lightbulbpress.com
Tel. 212-485-8800
ISBN: 978-1-933569-09-3

In the earlier editions of the *Guide to Personal Finance*, we explained the principles of making sound banking, credit, and mortgage decisions, as well as the basics of investing, financial planning, and taxes. Our goal was to be comprehensive without being exhaustive, informative without being overwhelming. Our focus was on what you should know, what you can expect to pay—and earn—and the pitfalls you should be aware of as you make financial decisions.

Those goals haven't altered, and neither has our approach. Since the last edition, however, there have been significant changes in the world of personal finance, giving people more choices but requiring more decision making. Online banking and investing have grown by leaps and bounds. Tax-free Roth IRAs and higher contribution limits for deductible traditional IRAs provide greater flexibility in retirement planning. Larger estates can be left to beneficiaries tax-free. To benefit from these changes, people have to know what they are and how to take advantage of them. That was one of our goals in bringing the *Guide* up to date.

This revised edition blends clear and concise information with visually appealing design—a style that's the trademark of Lightbulb Press.

We hope you enjoy the *Guide* and find it helpful and informative in exploring the often perplexing and ever-changing world of personal finance.

Virginia B. Morris
Kenneth M. Morris

GUIDE TO PERSONAL FINANCE

BANKING

CREDIT

HOME FINANCE

CONTENTS

FINANCIAL PLANNING

INVESTING

TAXES

Basics of Banking

The breathtaking pace of the banking evolution shows no sign of slowing down.

Managing your personal finances is a continual balancing act—keeping track of your earnings, paying your bills, and accumulating savings to pay for the things you need and want. For most people, it also involves having access to credit, including a credit card and loans to buy a home or a car.

Banks and credit unions can help you handle these tasks efficiently using insured checking and savings accounts. And, if you're looking for help with financial planning or making investments, most banks and credit unions offer these services too.

The reasons for working with a bank or credit union haven't changed very much since **automatic teller machines (ATMs)** were introduced in the 1970s. But over time the way you bank, and the way a bank delivers its services, have undergone a radical and largely digital transformation.

THE MAJOR PLAYERS

One of the primary challenges of banking is deciding where to open your accounts. In most parts of the country you have a large and varied choice. What you're looking for is the best combination of cost, convenience, and service that you can find, whether or not that means working with a single institution.

Commercial Banks

Local Banks

Large **commercial banks** that operate either nationwide or in relatively large geographic regions typically have the most branches, the widest range of accounts and services, and the most sophisticated technology. Most operate under a national bank charter and are regulated by the Federal Reserve and the Office of the Comptroller of the Currency (OCC).

Local banks serve a more limited community but offer many of the same services that larger banks do while charging lower fees and setting lower minimum balances. However, there may also be limitations, including fewer ATMs, less sophisticated electronic banking options, and fewer options for international money transfers. Most have the same federal oversight as larger banks, although some operate under state charters.

Credit unions are not-for-profit institutions owned by their depositors and are uniformly less expensive than for-profit banks. Each credit union sets its own membership requirements, and some are more restrictive than others. For example, you may have to work for a company to be eligible for its credit union. Large credit unions serve a national client base and offer the same services as large commercial banks, though some small credit unions may offer limited electronic banking, a short list of services, and few branches or ATM locations.

Virtual banks offer the same services as brick and mortar banks but exist only online. There are no branches and no proprietary ATMs. You transact all your business with them electronically, by computer or other digital device, though you can call to resolve questions or problems. A major advantage of virtual banks is that many provide low-cost or no-fee services, including rebates for ATM fees, as well as higher rates on savings accounts than more traditional banks offer.

ELECTRONIC BANKING

Even if your bank or credit union was built with traditional brick and mortar, employs tellers, and contains a vault full of safe-deposit boxes, most of the business you do there is handled electronically. So is everything that goes on behind the scenes, from direct deposits to your accounts to bill payment from them.

Even the paper checks you write are scanned to create digital images when they're deposited. The details are verified in real time and sent electronically to your bank through a Federal Reserve Bank or local clearinghouse. Then the amount is debited electronically from your account and credited to your payee's account—typically within a single business day.

Some elements of traditional banking do survive: You still have the option of making a deposit or withdrawal at a teller's window and talking to a bank officer in person about a specific request or problem. But that requires a trip to the bank and sometimes a wait in line.

LIKE MONEY IN THE BANK

Are banks the safest place to keep your money? The answer is an unequivocal yes.

The reason is the **Federal Deposit Insurance Corporation (FDIC)**. This federal agency guarantees depositors' balances up to $250,000 for each eligible account, including individual, joint, retirement, trust, and business accounts, in each participating bank.

Accounts with different banks are insured separately, and there's no cap on the total amount that qualifies for FDIC insurance provided that no one account holds more than $250,000. But, if you open similarly registered accounts in different branches of the same bank, they're considered one account for insurance purposes. The National Credit Union Administration (NCUA) provides identical insurance for accounts held in participating credit unions.

Remember, though, that FDIC or NCUA insurance applies only to deposits in checking or savings accounts, not to investments you buy through the bank or credit union.

Credit Unions

Virtual Banks

THE SERVICES BANKS PROVIDE

Here's a quick summary of primary banking services:

- **Checking and savings accounts**
- **Certificates of deposits and money market accounts**
- **Direct deposit and check cashing**
- **Online bill payment**
- **Account-linked bank or debit cards**
- **Credit cards and other lines of credit**
- **Mortgages and personal loans**
- **Money transfers**

WHEN A BANK ISN'T A BANK

Non-bank banks, also called non-bank financial institutions, offer banking services but are not actually banks because they are not licensed or supervised by national or state banking authorities. The specific services they provide vary from company to company, which range from hedge funds and giant warehouse stores to small check-cashing operations. Using their services may be—but aren't necessarily—convenient and cost-effective. What's more, the lack of regulation may mean you have limited consumer protections.

Checking Accounts

You pay your bills with a checking account even if you rarely write a check.

When you pay a bill from your bank account, you're using what's known as a **demand deposit** or **transaction account**. Demand means that your money is available when you want it, without giving the bank prior notice. Transaction means that you can tell the bank to transfer money from your account to another account. You're the **payer** in this situation and the person or institution you're paying is the **payee**.

Whether you use a paper check, computer, tablet, or mobile phone, you must provide the same information:

- The name of the payee
- The amount you want transferred
- Your authorization, using either a handwritten or electronic signature

Most of the other information that's imprinted on a paper check—the bank routing number, your account number, and the number of the check—is built into the bank's bill-pay program.

Timing checks to make sure your payments arrive on time requires some planning whichever way you pay. With a paper check, unless you pay in person, you have to allow time for mail delivery, which can vary by region and distance. If you pay electronically, you can schedule the date the payment is made, but you may still have to allow two or three days for the electronic funds to transfer, or longer if your bank is sending a paper check because the payee doesn't accept electronic payments.

ACH WHO?

Most electronic payments you authorize from your checking account move to your payee's account through an **automated clearinghouse (ACH)**, or electronic network operated by the Federal Reserve Banks. That's the case whether you authorize payments as they are due or schedule payments on a regular basis, such as installments on a mortgage or car loan or your monthly electric bill.

Deposits into your account, including your paycheck and payments from government programs such as Social Security, are also handled though the ACH network.

ACH deposits are available either on the day they are paid to your account or the next business day. The same timing applies to cash deposits but often not to paper checks you deposit. The bank may make a portion of the check amount available the day of deposit but hold the full amount for several days, depending on the source of the check. National banks are required to credit your account with the full amount in no longer than five business days—though there are some exceptions, including new accounts and deposits over $5,000.

WHEN YOU CAN WITHDRAW

Funds may be available on a slightly different schedule at each bank. Here's one example of when you might be able to withdraw after depositing different types of checks, each for $1,000. Your bank should display the schedule it uses or make a copy available.

	1 day later	2 days later	5 days later
A federal, state, or local government check*	$1,000		
A bank, certified, or travelers check	$1,000		
A check from your own bank	$1,000		
A local check	$100	$400	$500
A non-local check	$100		$900

*Special deposit ticket may be required.

NONSUFFICIENT FUNDS

ACCOUNT BALANCE

$0

OVERDRAFT

Banks follow your payment instructions, whether they're given in writing or electronically, provided there is money available in your account to cover the amount. But if you're short, even if you've deposited money that hasn't yet been fully credited to your account, you'll face a potential problem variously known as an overdraft, nonsufficient funds (NSF), insufficient funds, or in some cases unavailable funds. Informally it's called bouncing a check.

If the bank refuses to pay your debit, as it could, you'll owe an overdraft fee and the payee's bank will almost certainly charge a similar fee. What's more, if a payment is returned for insufficient funds, you may face a late-payment fee and an interest charge from the payee.

In addition to keeping careful track of your available balance so you don't encounter this situation, you can often arrange **overdraft protection** linked to your account. In most cases this is a special line of credit from which the bank automatically transfers money to your account to cover overdrafts. You must pay interest on the amount that's transferred as well as repay the balance, and there may also be a penalty fee each time you access the credit. In the long run, though, overdraft protection can save time, money, and major inconvenience.

Your bank may not automatically offer overdraft protection when you open a new account, but you should ask how to qualify. Some basic accounts don't offer it at all, but many accounts do. So its availability may be a factor in deciding where to open your checking account.

STOP THAT PAYMENT

When you send a paper check, you can ask the bank to stop payment, which means it should refuse to honor the check when it is deposited. If you make your request in writing before the check has been cashed, your bank will usually do as you ask although it may charge a substantial fee. A stop payment order remains in effect for 60 days.

Electronic payments generally can't be stopped once you have authorized them. But if you have authorized a recurring debit from your account, you can generally end the arrangement by notifying the bank in writing three days before the next debit is scheduled to occur.

If debits that have revoked continue to be honored, notify the bank in writing within 60 days from the time you get your bank statement that reports the debit. The bank must investigate within ten days.

You can also file a complaint with the Consumer Financial Protection Bureau (www.consumerfinance.gov) if it's a national bank, with the National Credit Union Administration (www.ncua.gov), or your state banking department.

CHECK SHORTCUTS

Instead of returning cancelled paper checks, most banks provide electronic reproductions, reduced-size images, or simply a list of items that were paid in your monthly statement. If you need a copy of a check as legal proof of payment, you should request a substitute check, which has the words "This is a legal copy…" printed on it. But be prepared to pay a fee. Most, though not all, banks charge for this service.

Opening an Account

Costs and features vary enormously, so it pays to check around.

Most banks offer several types of checking accounts to meet the needs—and attract the business—of potential customers.

In most cases, the best account for you is the one that will cost you the least to manage your finances efficiently. But that's not always the cheapest account—or the one with the most services. To choose wisely, you need to be clear about the services you need.

Many banks have an account designed specifically for students and another for seniors. These tend to cost less than regular accounts, though they may have some limitations. In addition, some states require banks to offer a lower-cost but barebones account to help make banking available to everyone.

THE PRICE OF BANKING

Cost is a major factor in choosing one bank over another, assuming both offer comparable services. Cost may also be the driving force in switching banks.

In most cases, the key expense is a checking account, including access to traditional and electronic bill payments, unlimited ATM use, and a debit card. A monthly fee may cover all those features, but there may be a combination of monthly fee plus additional charges for transactions over a limited number.

The good news is that it's possible to find a bank that includes these services without charge in exchange for keeping at least a minimum balance in your account and having your paycheck direct deposited. The bank may describe this arrangement as free checking, but, given the minimum balance requirement, that's not exactly the case. You'll also discover that virtual banks generally offer free checking without minimum deposits.

CHECK THE FEES

You'll probably want to pay particular attention to ATM charges if you use cash machines regularly. Some banks charge a fee—often $1 or $2, but sometimes more—every time you withdraw or check your balance, and most banks charge a fee when you use a terminal it doesn't own. A better arrangement, often part of a free checking account, allows unlimited use of a bank's own terminals as well as those within a regional, national, or even international network, such as NYCE, Cirrus, STAR, and Plus.

Other fees may apply as well, to cover:

- Overdrafts, also known as nonsufficient funds (NSF)
- Money orders and bank checks
- Stop payment orders
- Check printing

Some banks have experimented with fees for talking to a teller or using your debit card and may revisit them again.

The bank must explain its fee structure in writing and notify you whenever there are changes, but the details are often imbedded in the fine print of the client account materials you receive. That's why it is important to keep up to date on the costs and to question any charges that seem wrong to you.

The real catch is that checking fees vary not only from bank to bank but among account types at the same bank. So you may have to investigate carefully to find the least expensive option that meets your needs.

MINIMUM BALANCES

A minimum balance is the least amount of money you must keep on deposit in your account to satisfy a bank's requirement, and can range from $500 to $15,000.

Some banks figure your average monthly minimum balance, which means you can meet the minimum even if your balance dips below that required level at some point during the month. Other banks charge the fee if your balance drops below the minimum at any point. You should always know which method your bank uses so you can avoid low balance fees.

Often, though not always, you can meet the minimum using the combined average of all your accounts: checking, savings, certificates of deposit (CDs), and sometimes even outstanding loans.

There are two cautions: Meeting minimum balance requirements can save you money on bank fees. But you'll want to compare what you would save on fees with what you could earn by investing the money you're using to meet the minimum elsewhere. And you'll want to be careful not to choose an account with a minimum you'll have to struggle to meet. The penalty charges you're likely to incur could cost you a lot.

TAKE A TIP

Here are some things to think about before you choose a new checking account:

- The number of transactions, including ATM withdrawals, you have each month. The more there are, the more flexible an account you'll need.
- The way you pay most bills. If you prefer electronic banking, be sure the bank's programs are state-of-the-art.
- The special services you may need, such as bank checks or signature guarantees. In this case you may need a local bank in addition to a virtual one.
- How much you travel, domestically and internationally. You may be better off using a major bank with lots of ATMs.

SHOP AROUND

The best place to start your search for checking accounts is online, focusing on banks and credit unions near your home or office as well as those of virtual banks. Then follow up on the ones that seem most promising.

One caution: be sure the sources you're using to conduct your search are current and impartial, not promotions from a specific institution. And check with family, friends, and others you respect to find out what their banking experiences have been. If you're having trouble finding credit unions, contact the Credit Union National Association (CUNA) at www.cuna.org.

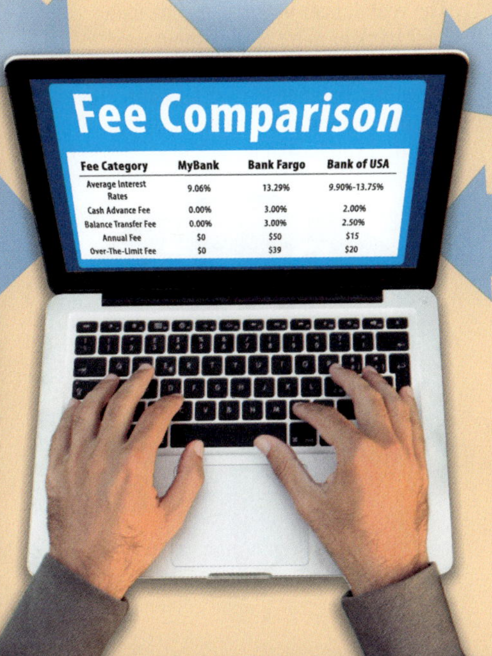

Fee Category	MyBank	Bank Fargo	Bank of USA
Average Interest Rates	9.06%	13.29%	9.90%-13.75%
Cash Advance Fee	0.00%	3.00%	2.00%
Balance Transfer Fee	0.00%	3.00%	2.50%
Annual Fee	$0	$50	$15
Over-The-Limit Fee	$0	$39	$20

Banking by Card

ATM withdrawals were only the start of electronic banking.

When you go to the bank, you're likely to use the ATM to make a withdrawal, deposit, or electronic payment on your credit card or bank loan. Or you might simply check your account balance.

And when you pay for a purchase, chances are you swipe, dip, or wave a plastic card or use an app on your smartphone. In many cases, the card is linked directly to your bank account and transfers the amount you spend from your account to the payee's account.

One reason that paying this way is so attractive is that if you're careful to keep your spending in line with your account balance—and don't overdraw—you don't have to worry about accumulating debt, which is always a risk with a credit card.

NON-IDENTICAL TWINS

The card that gives you direct access to your checking account may be a **bank card** or a **debit card**. They're not identical. The bank card gives you access to ATMs and allows you to make point-of-sale (POS) purchases using your personal identification number (PIN). A debit card can be used this way but additionally to make purchases by signing your name or providing the number online or by phone, with no PIN required.

How can you tell the difference between the two? A debit card, sometimes called a check card, has a VISA or MasterCard logo as well as the bank name and logo. A bank card, sometimes called an ATM card, has just the bank identification.

HOW THE CARDS WORK

There are generally no limits on the number of transactions you can authorize in a day, though banks may set a daily dollar limit on ATM withdrawals and card purchases. At some banks the amount you can spend is equal to the amount you can withdraw as cash, for example, $500 in each category. Other banks set a single daily limit.

If you want overdraft protection with your bank or debit card, you must agree to allow the bank to provide it. The advantage is that you won't be inconvenienced or embarrassed by having a transaction rejected. But the reason to decline is that you limit the risk of overspending or incurring overdraft fees and interest payments, which can be substantial.

Bank Card

- Access to ATM
- POS purchase using PIN

WHICH CARD FOR YOU?
While debit cards can be handy, a bank card may be a smarter choice. Among other things, it is less vulnerable to abuse, since the card is worthless to a thief or fraudster without your PIN.

PROTECTING YOUR MONEY

The real danger is that someone using your bank or debit card without your permission could potentially withdraw the entire balance in your account, plus the full amount of your overdraft line of credit, if you have one.

Debit Card

- **Access to ATM**
- **POS purchase using PIN**
- **POS purchase using signature, phone, and online**

But the law is on your side, specifically the Federal Reserve Board's Regulation E (Reg E), which governs all electronic fund transfers (EFTs). The bottom line is that if you notify your bank that your card is missing or that money has been fraudulently withdrawn from your account within two business days of making the discovery, the most you can lose is $50. In fact, many banks will refund the entire amount, including the $50.

Of course, if you have made a number of payments against what you thought was an adequate balance, those payments may be returned for insufficient funds. That's a separate problem you'll have to resolve.

THE TICKING CLOCK

Reg E is flexible on the two-day rule. You don't have to report the card missing within 48 hours of the actual loss, since it's entirely possible you may not discover that it's gone right away. In fact, you have 60 days from the postmark on the bank statement that reports the loss or misuse.

As long as you're within the time limit, you still won't lose more than $50.

But if you miss the deadline, you could be out up to $500 of any amounts withdrawn during those 60 days plus anything and everything that's withdrawn beginning on the 61st day.

Your bank initially has ten days to investigate your report and refund any money it agrees was withdrawn without your permission. If it wishes, the bank can extend the investigation for up to 45 days. But if you've filed a written report, it must put the disputed amount back into your account within ten business days so you won't be out the money.

The bank has more flexibility with accounts open less than 30 days. It can take 20 days to finish the initial inquiry and refund your money, and up to 90 days for an extended investigation. If the bank believes the evidence doesn't support your claims, getting a loss resolved can be time-consuming and potentially costly.

FEE, FIE

If you pay by bank or debit card, retailers have the right to add a transaction fee to your bill. Any charge should be clearly stated, so you can decide if the convenience is worth the cost. Be especially alert when you use an ATM in a non-bank setting. Those fees can be outrageous.

A WORD OF WARNING

A potential problem may occur if you use a debit card to charge certain expenses, such as gas or hotel rooms, where the cost is not fixed. In that case, the retailer debits your account twice, first to hold the amount that you might spend and a second time for the actual amount you spent. It can take several days for the first charge to be credited back to your account, potentially putting you in an overdraft situation.

Payment Systems

Finding a convenient way to pay is rarely a problem.

You may be satisfied with the bill payment options your bank offers. But if you're looking for other ways to pay—and be paid—you shouldn't have any trouble finding an alternative. In fact, you may want to investigate several.

PAYEE REQUESTS

Rather than using your bank's bill-pay software, you can authorize your payees to debit your checking account when a payment is due. Direct debit assures that your payment is made on time even though the amount may not be transferred from your account immediately.

Just be sure, when you authorize a debit in this way, to record the confirmation number that appears on the payee's website and hold onto it until the statement reflecting payment arrives.

Authorizing debits requires you to share your bank account number, something that may make you uneasy. When payees are reputable institutions, such as the banks that issue the credit cards you use, your wireless telephone provider, or the company that financed the purchase of your car, there's virtually no chance that your account will be at risk. But you want to exercise caution in making your banking account information more widely available, just as you would with sharing your Social Security number.

You may also want to be careful before you schedule recurring payments, especially those where the amount varies from month to month. Preauthorizing a debit of an unusually large payment could risk overdrawing your account. In addition, if you authorize each payment separately, especially in the case of credit cards, you can decide how much to pay each month. With a prescheduled debit, the only options may be paying only the full balance or the minimum amount due.

POP GOES THE MONEY

Popmoney, which describes itself as a personal payment service, lets you make or receive person-to-person payments, pay bills, or make gifts electronically, using your existing checking, savings, or money market account.

Payers must provide an email address, mobile phone number, or bank information for the payee so the transfer can be made. There is a mechanism for refunding transactions that can't be completed—for example if the payee doesn't respond—but payers are responsible for providing correct contact information.

The service is free for recipients, while senders may or may not pay a fee, depending on where they bank. But there are limitations. There are daily and monthly dollar transfer limits, the service works only within the United States, and at least three days elapse between authorizing a payment and completing a transaction—though real-time payments may be available through banks that offer the option.

For more information, or if your bank doesn't participate, you can contact www.popmoney.com. There's also a Popmoney service for small businesses.

popmoney

A WARNING
Preauthorized debts can be a bad idea in cases when a payee is not scrupulously honest and continues to debit your account against your wishes. While it is legally possible to terminate such an arrangement, it may not be as easy as it should be. In some cases, banks have been faulted for profiting from abusive debit payments.

PREPAID DEBIT CARDS

You can use a prepaid debit card any place you can use a regular debit card. The difference between the two is that the amount you can spend is loaded onto the prepaid card rather than debited directly from a linked account.

The advantage of using a prepaid card is that it's much harder to overspend. That's because you have no overdraft option. But the potential risk is that some cards carry fees that consume a substantial portion of the amounts loaded on them. So investigate fees carefully before you choose a prepaid card and confirm that your balance will be refunded if your card is lost or stolen.

PAYPAL

You can use PayPal to pay for purchases, be paid for something you sell, or send money to another person, all while guarding the privacy of your personal financial information. Buying is free, and so is transferring money, provided you send it from a linked bank account or a PayPal account. If you transfer money using a debit or credit card, you pay the same fee that you do when you sell. Fees on international transactions are higher.

PayPal describes itself as a digital wallet where you can link your various financial accounts, including banking, debit, and credit arrangements, to a PayPal account and choose the one you'll use to make a payment. The privacy feature, which means, among other things, that you never have to share your credit card or bank account number, is a major attraction.

PayPal isn't a bank, does not insure the money in your PayPal account, and isn't regulated by any federal or state authority. And not everyone is happy with its service. There have been glitches over the years, and banks provide some services that PayPal doesn't. But there's no question that PayPal is a major force in the world of electronic money.

BITCOIN

Bitcoin is one of the most controversial payment options in the still-evolving world of digital currency. This software enables person-to-person transactions worldwide using metaphorical electronic wallets.

Bitcoin payments you receive can be converted to local currency. But because bitcoin is not a fiat currency whose value is established by an issuing government, it doesn't have a fixed value and can be volatile. And as the website www.bitcoin.org warns, it's a high-risk asset that's not suitable for savings. You may not be ready to use it right now, but it's probably worth learning more about.

Tracking Your Balance

You need to stay current on what's in your checking account.

It's easier than ever to keep track of the activity in your checking account. The details of each credit and debit transaction, the type of transaction it was, and the current balance are available online all the time. Regularly scheduled debits that are due but have not yet been paid may be listed as pending.

Once a month, though not always at the end of the month, activity in your account is compiled in a statement that may be mailed to you, can be downloaded as a PDF file, or both. Statements going back several months or longer are also available, but you may have to request that they be retrieved from the archives.

While there is sometimes a fee for checking your account balance at an ATM, it's easy—and free—to access your account balance online or from your mobile phone. That means you should never tap your overdraft line of credit accidently or have a withdrawal refused for insufficient funds. But you do have to make the effort to check on a regular basis.

CHECKBOOK RECORDS

If you still use paper checks, your checkbook will have a recordkeeping system, whether as a separate ledger, stubs attached to the checks, or a carbon-copy of the checks you write. None of these is especially useful for keeping a running tally of your account if you also make electronic payments. But they can be helpful in confirming that you have, in fact, written checks to specific payees and that the amount of each check is accurately reflected in your statement or online account details.

GETTING IT WRONG

You're not likely to find many mistakes in bank statements. But you should regularly compare your own records—such as ATM and debit card receipts and regular direct deposits of your paycheck or other income—to what your account details or monthly statement show, since mistakes can happen. Generally you have 60 days to report problems with electronic fund transfers (EFTs), but only 14 days for other types of errors. The sooner you notify the bank, the better. And always follow up a verbal report with a written one.

What's more likely to happen is that your sense of what's in your account is different from what the bank detail shows. If you've underestimated your account balance, which probably doesn't happen very often, it may be that you've forgotten about deposits you've made, especially as deposit slips have become extinct.

If you chronically overestimate your balance, however, chances are you need to

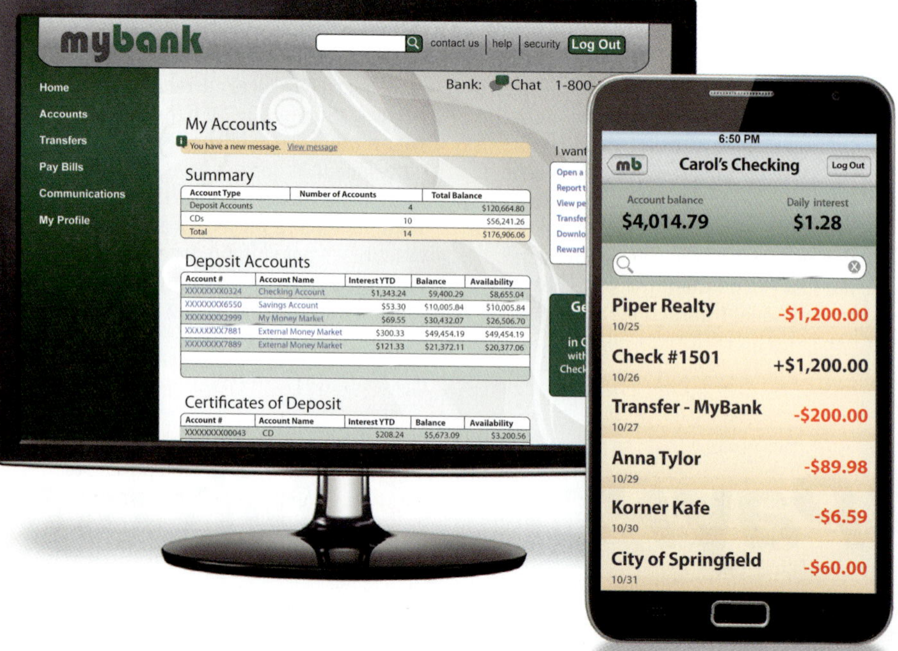

pay more attention to what you're spending, especially if you pay for most purchases, even small ones, with plastic and don't keep the receipts.

PAYROLL CARDS

Some employers use payroll cards to pay salary or wages, either instead of, or in addition to, direct deposits to your bank account or paper paychecks. Some payroll cards provide monthly statements that:

- Allow you to track your spending
- Limit the number of fees
- Provide FDIC insurance and reimbursement of remaining balances if the card is lost or stolen, though you may have to pay for a replacement card

But all cards are not created equal. Some have fewer consumer protections and higher fees. And some seem downright predatory: They may include charges for inactivity fees, for all ATM withdrawals after the first or second one in a month, and for each purchase you make.

If your only option is a payroll card, and the fees are eating up too much of your pay, you should complain to the Consumer Financial Protection Bureau at www.consumerfinance.gov and your elected representatives. The purpose of payroll cards is not to create a financial drain on employees.

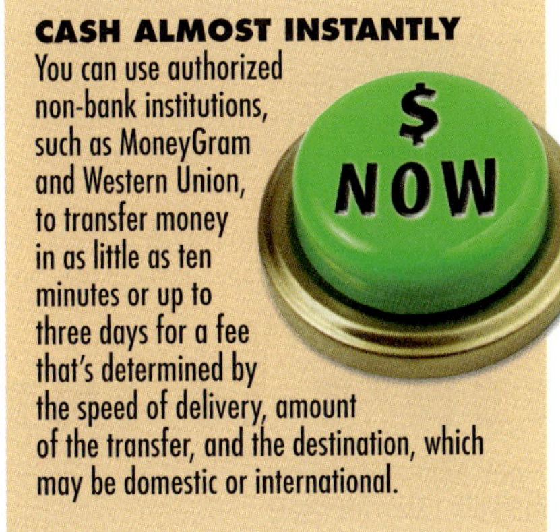

CASH ALMOST INSTANTLY

You can use authorized non-bank institutions, such as MoneyGram and Western Union, to transfer money in as little as ten minutes or up to three days for a fee that's determined by the speed of delivery, amount of the transfer, and the destination, which may be domestic or international.

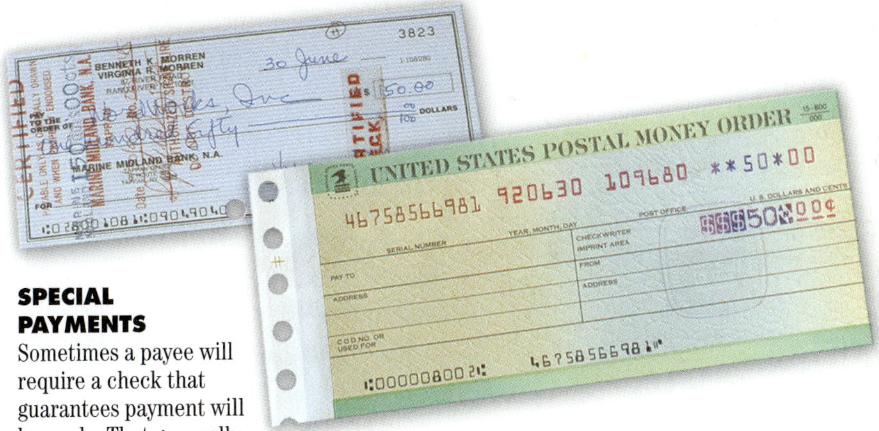

SPECIAL PAYMENTS

Sometimes a payee will require a check that guarantees payment will be made. That generally means having a personal check certified or using a bank check or money order.

When you write a certified check, your bank puts a hold on the amount of the check, and stamps ***certified*** on the face. There's no limit on the amount of the check, provided you have enough money in your account to cover it. When it's cashed, the amount is debited and shows up in your bank statement.

To arrange for a bank check, you tell the bank teller how much the check should be for and who the payee is. You then either write a check to the bank or debit the amount from your account. The check, which comes with a carbon copy for your records, is machine printed and signed by a bank officer.

The same is true of a money order, which you can purchase from a bank or a post office. The fee is often higher at a bank, but the limits on the amount of the money order are also higher.

With all these guaranteed payments, once the document has been sent or given to the payee, you can't stop payment. And with bank checks and money orders, there is no confirmation in your bank statement or elsewhere that payment has been made.

Savings

Putting money away for a rainy day is the basic idea behind savings accounts.

Bank **deposit accounts**, better known as savings accounts, pay interest on the principal, or balance in your account, to encourage you to keep your money in the bank—although you don't earn all that much even in periods when rates are high. When rates are low, earnings are essentially nonexistent.

But savings accounts are important to your financial security, and the way you use them best is by adding to them on a regular basis, every week or every month, so you accumulate a substantial balance.

Among their primary benefits are that they:

- Provide a safe place to accumulate money for your short-term goals
- Work well as rainy day and emergency funds

The Truth in Savings Act requires all banks to disclose the annual percentage yield (APY) you would earn and fees you would pay clearly so you can make an informed comparison.

ISN'T IT INTERESTING?

When banks advertise interest rates for their savings accounts, they include the **nominal rate** and the **annual percentage yield (APY)**. The nominal, or named, rate is the rate they pay. The APY is what you earn over a year, in dollars and cents, expressed as a percentage of your principal.

The nominal rate, which won't vary much from bank to bank at any given time, depends on what banks are earning on the loans they make and on what it costs them to borrow from each other, both of which are affected by the monetary policy the Federal Reserve Bank is following. When borrowing is expensive, you earn a little more on your savings. When borrowing costs are low, you earn less.

The APY depends on the interest rate the bank pays and the compounding method it uses. When interest compounds, it is added to the existing principal to become the new base on which the next interest payment is figured. The higher the rate and the more often it compounds, the greater the yield.

PLUSES OF SAVINGS ACCOUNTS

- Handy way to accumulate money for short-term goals, emergencies
- Money in a savings account can reduce — or eliminate — charges on your checking account
- Bank savings are FDIC-insured for up to $250,000 per depositor for several different types of accounts

MINUSES OF SAVINGS ACCOUNTS

- Other kinds of accounts, such as CDs and money market funds, pay more — sometimes much more — interest
- Most banks discourage small savings accounts by not paying interest below a minimum balance and/or by charging service fees that can erode the interest you earn, actually costing you money to save

FIGURING INTEREST

Some savings accounts, including money market accounts, may pay different rates of interest on different balances or different segments of your total balance. If the rate is **tiered**, you earn the highest rate on your entire balance once you meet the minimum. If it is **blended**, you earn different rates.

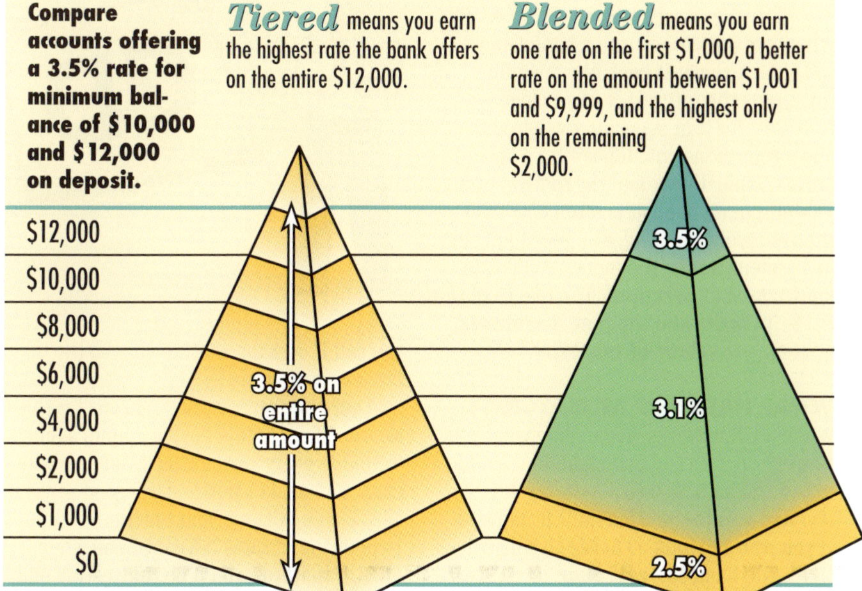

TYPES OF ACCOUNTS

Bank and credit union savings accounts generally come in three varieties: regular savings, also called statement accounts, money market accounts, and certificates of deposit (CDs). All are similarly insured but differ from each other in certain ways.

Regular accounts earn interest at the lowest rate but have the fewest restrictions. You can withdraw when you like or transfer money to another account in your name. What you can't do is pay a third party directly from the account.

Money market accounts are hybrids, combining some checking account features in a savings account. Specifically, you can write up to three checks or make three electronic transfers to a third party each statement period—typically a month. You earn interest at a higher rate than on regular savings, provided you always keep the required minimum balance on deposit. Otherwise you may lose interest and owe a fee.

CDs are time deposits, which means you must leave your money on deposit for the term to which you agree or pay a penalty by forfeiting interest. CDs typically earn the highest rates of any bank account, but they can never be used as transaction accounts.

ACCUMULATING SAVINGS

There's no golden rule establishing how much you should be saving, but aiming for 10% of your gross income is a good place to start. If you can boost it to 15%, that's even better. Anything you're contributing to a retirement savings plan at work counts toward the total. And whenever you get a bonus or other cash payment, it's smart to save at least some of it.

If you're saving for a specific goal, find out what it will cost and divide the total by the number of months remaining before you need the money. That will tell you how much you have to save each month. Because there's a tangible reward for the effort you're making, saving may be easier.

It may also help you to save regularly if you have a fixed amount direct deposited from your paycheck to a savings account rather than having the full amount go into checking. If that's not possible, you can always arrange a regular debit from your checking to your savings account.

SAFE-DEPOSIT BOXES

Safe-deposit boxes are designed for keeping important papers and objects such as deeds, jewelry, birth and marriage certificates, plus a list of your valuable possessions. Most banks rent them for anywhere from $15 to several hundred a year, depending on size.

However, you can use the box only during regular banking hours. And the box may be sealed if you die, limiting access to valuables for your surviving family — including your spouse — until your will is legally filed.

CD: Certificate of Deposit

CDs are popular investments because they live up to their promise of safety.

When you put money into a bank CD, you expect to get it back at a specific time, plus the interest it has earned. In return for that security, you agree to leave your money on deposit for a specific period, typically six months to five years. The minimum deposit is often $500, but there's rarely a ceiling, or upper limit. In investment terms, the money you put in is known as your **principal**. The length of the CD is its **term**, and the time it **matures**, or ends, is its **date of maturity**.

WHAT HAPPENS AT MATURITY

When a CD matures, you decide what you want to do with the principal, but you have to tell the bank in writing what you've decided within the time limit it imposes. If you wait too long or never give instructions, the bank can **roll over**, or reinvest, your CD for the same term but at the going rate.

You might ask for a rollover in any case, but if you need the money, or if the new rate will be lower than the interest you've been earning or that you could earn on a different investment, you might decide to get out of CDs. In that case, the bank can **sweep**, or move, the money into another of your accounts, wire transfer it to another bank for a fee, or send you a check.

BUILDING A LADDER

One smart approach to buying CDs is using a technique known as **laddering**. Instead of putting a large sum into a single CD with a specific term, you split your principal into three or more CDs that mature in a stepped pattern—perhaps every six months over an 18-month period. Each time a CD matures, you roll it over for another year so the ladder continues.

There are several good reasons for this approach, including having a lump sum available every six months if you need the cash. This makes particularly good sense if you're using CDs as your emergency fund. In addition, if rates have dropped when one CD matures, you'll be reinvesting only a portion of the total at the lower rate.

STRATEGIC CHOICES

You can choose CDs from any insured bank or credit union and be confident that your money is safe. What you have to decide is what makes the most financial sense for you. You may find that an online bank pays a higher rate and decide to put your money there. Or, if your bank requires a minimum balance for free checking and

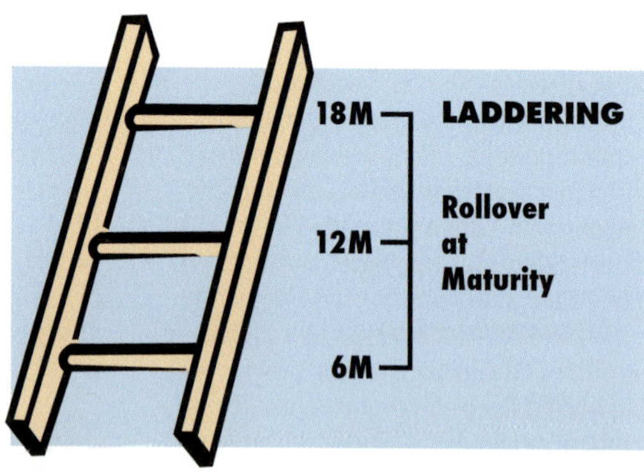

REWARDS OF CDs

- The yield is higher than on other bank accounts
- Knowing what you'll have and when you can take it out lets you plan for future cash needs
- You can choose a term that's suited to your financial goals
- You pay no charges for a bank CD
- Changing economic conditions do not reduce what you earn on an existing CD
- Your CD is insured by the FDIC or NCUA

other services, you may conclude that using at least some of your CD principal to maintain that level is smart.

Additionally, when interest rates are low, it's probably best to concentrate on relatively short-term CDs so that you're in a better position to take advantage of rising rates in the future.

THE LANGUAGE OF CDs

You can make wiser decisions about CDs when you're comfortable with what some key words mean.

Yield is the amount you earn in interest during a year, expressed as a percentage of the principal. It's often reported as annual percentage yield (APY).

Interest rate is the percentage of principal added to your CD to produce the yield. If the interest compounds, the APY will be higher than the interest rate. With most CDs, the rate is **fixed**. With others it may be **flexible**, or could change although there is usually a floor limiting how low it can go. **Floating** rates are pegged, or linked, to a published interest rate, such as that on a US Treasury note, and go up or down as that rate changes.

Compounding occurs when the interest you earn is added to the principal, forming a new base on which future interest is calculated. Interest may compound daily, monthly, quarterly, or some longer period.

USING CDs

If you have regular expenses, like tuition payments, or anticipate a large cost at a specific time, you can time your CDs to come due when you need the money. Banks may be flexible, too, if you ask for a special term. For example, if you are planning to buy a house in seven months, you may be able to get a custom seven-month CD at a better rate than a regular six-month variety.

HOW COMPOUNDING WORKS

You can see how compounding increases the value of your savings in the example below, where interest is added quarterly:

First quarter	**Base amount** **+ Interest**
Second quarter	**= New base amount** **+ Interest**
Third quarter	**= New base amount** **+ Interest**
Fourth quarter	**= New base amount** **+ Interest**
	= Value after one year

RISKS OF CDs

- Your money is locked in at a specific rate, even if interest rates go up
- You will probably lose some or all interest that has accumulated if you take your money out early
- You may earn more with other non-bank options
- The new interest rate may be lower when you reinvest, or roll over, your CD
- If your bank is taken over by another bank, your CD term or rate may change

Using Credit

When you borrow money to pay for something or use a card to charge a purchase, you're using credit.

Using **credit** means being able to buy the things or services you need or want by borrowing the money to pay for them. When you arrange for credit, you agree to repay the lender the amount you have borrowed. You typically pay a finance charge, calculated as a percentage of the amount you borrowed, for the opportunity to use the credit.

Loans and **lines of credit**, of which **credit cards** are the best-known example, are the types of credit people use most often. Loans allow you to borrow a specific amount as a lump sum and repay over time. Lines of credit give you revolving access to a fixed sum of money. Revolving means that as soon as you repay what you have borrowed, you can borrow it again.

AVAILABLE CREDIT

Creditors are willing, and often eager, to advance you the **principal**, or money you borrow, because they make money on the finance charges you pay, especially if you stretch out the payments over an extended period. Creditors figure the **finance charge** by adding a percentage of the principal to the amount you owe.

Principal
+ % Interest
= Finance Charges

The percentage, called the **interest rate**, varies, depending on the type of credit you're using and the amount of competition the creditor has in attracting your business. It's often linked to the interest rates that are current in the economy at large, particularly the **prime rate**, which lenders use as a benchmark rate. In general, finance charges on credit cards are figured at a higher—sometimes much higher—rate than the rates on most loans.

Other factors sometimes influence the finance charges you pay, including your credit reputation or assumptions a potential creditor makes about you. If a creditor believes there's a risk that you may **default**, or fail to repay, the rate you'll have to pay for credit may be higher than someone who seems to pose less risk.

EVALUATING CREDIT USE

People use credit in different ways. Some of their choices work better than others.

Credit cards can be a convenient way to simplify bill-paying. If you charge a number of different purchases, you can make a single payment. If you regularly pay in full and on time, there's usually no finance charge. And you may accumulate rewards points if your card offers such a program. You may also be able to take advantage of sales, avoid carrying large sums of cash, or shop conveniently by phone or online.

On the other hand, if you regularly charge more than you can afford to pay, the finance charges can add substantially to your expenses, and in the worst of circumstances drive you deeply into debt.

Similarly, a car loan or lease can enable you to replace an old car with one less apt to need expensive repairs. But you can also find yourself repaying a loan on a car or other property that's no longer serviceable. Or worse yet, if you over-commit yourself and can't pay, you may lose the property entirely.

CREDIT PARTNERS

Two parties are involved in making credit work, the **consumer**, or user of credit, and the **creditor**, or supplier of credit. And unless you have informal arrangements with family or friends, getting credit usually involves an agreement you make with a financial institution such as a bank or a credit union.

ARTHUR MORRIS originated the installment loan. His Morris Plan, the first to make credit available to the average citizen, began in 1916 despite common wisdom that lending money to working people was doomed to failure. Today, it's hard to imagine how the US economy could function without credit.

Customarily, the partners agree on the amount of credit available and the conditions under which it will be repaid, as well as the fee the creditor will charge for advancing the money. Since credit is a common phenomenon, those agreements are generally standardized. But that doesn't mean that the terms are identical from issuer to issuer. It's important to understand what the credit will cost, expressed as an **annual percentage rate (APR)**, and to do some comparison shopping. After all, any creditor to which you apply will check whether you're a good risk before making money available to you.

CREDIT REGULATION

Legitimate credit providers are regulated by the US government and the states where they operate. The laws, which have evolved over time, require the lenders to offer credit on an equal basis, disclose credit terms and conditions, and avoid unfair and deceptive practices, including hidden fees and unreasonable expenses. The law also governs liability for unauthorized use of your credit card and details procedures for resolving billing errors and other disputes.

Among the problems that need greater regulation is marketing of expensive and unnecessary add-on services, like identity theft protection and credit monitoring.

TWO FACES OF CREDIT

Credit has enabled many people to live better by paying for goods or services as part of their regular living expenses rather than having to wait until they could afford to make the purchase. It's more available today to a broader range of people than it customarily was in the past.

In fact, most Americans use credit in one form or another: About 80% of US households have credit cards, most people who buy homes have a mortgage loan, and about 60% of college students (or their parents) use loans to help pay tuition.

But credit does have a downside. Although many people use credit wisely, some owe more than they are able to repay. It may be that they've used credit to buy food and gas as usual but have lost their jobs or are burdened by major medical expenses. It may be that they've been unrealistic about what they can afford, or that they haven't recognized how deeply in debt they are. Whatever the reason, the consequences are costly and put access to future credit at risk.

Credit Cards

Access to revolving credit doesn't have to make your head spin.

When you apply for a credit card, you sign an agreement with the card issuer—usually but not always a bank—to repay amounts you borrow against your **credit limit**, a dollar amount that the issuer sets. Each time you make a purchase you reduce the amount of credit available. But amounts you repay are applied to the credit limit and available to borrow again.

For example, if you have a credit limit of $3,500 and charge purchases of $1,500, your available credit is $2,000. If you repay the full amount, your available credit returns to $3,500. If you repay $500 instead, your available credit is $2,500.

This revolving cycle of borrowing, repaying, and borrowing again can continue indefinitely as long as you pay at least the minimum you owe on time.

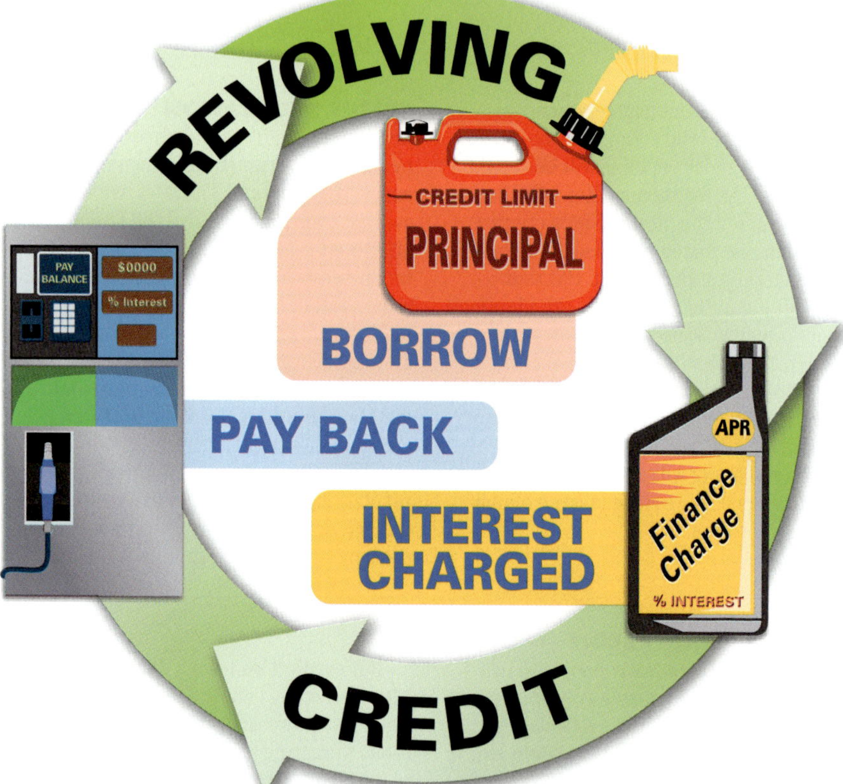

THE CREDIT CYCLE

Every credit card has 12 billing periods that end on or about the same date every month—though that date varies from card to card. When the period ends, the card issuer prepares a statement that details all of your purchases and credits since the previous statement, calculates your outstanding balance, and sets the minimum payment and the payment date. The payment date must be the same date every month and at least 21 days after the bill is posted online or mailed to you.

Your statement will tell you when the billing period ends, or closes. That's handy information, because you can time a major purchase for just after the closing date and take advantage of a credit float. That means you won't have to pay for purchase until the following statement's due date—generally about seven weeks in the future.

THE COST OF CREDIT

It's true that you may pay more for buying with a credit card than you would if you paid cash. That's the cost of convenience. But the additional cost of using revolving credit—if there is one—depends on how you pay your bill.

If you've paid your previous bill in full and on time, and you do so again, the credit costs you nothing—provided your card has a grace period. A **grace period** allows card users who have paid their previous balance in full to avoid interest on purchases made during the current billing cycle. Cards aren't required to provide a grace period, but if you regularly pay on time it's worth looking for one that does.

GRACE PERIOD

However, if you pay only part of your outstanding balance, you owe interest on the unpaid amount. You also owe interest on any purchases during the month beginning on the day of the purchase. The most common method for calculating the amount of interest you owe is based on the daily outstanding balance in your account, with this amount compounding daily.

Your billing statement includes a chart with a warning about how much interest you'll owe if you pay over three years or pay only the required minimum. The latter is not a pretty picture—and the calculation assumes you don't use the card for additional purchases. If you go on spending, the problem gets worse.

If you want to see what it would cost you to repay an outstanding balance by making minimum payments, check out the credit card calculator at www.federalreserve.gov. For example, assuming you owed $5,400 with an APR of 18%, it would take you 36 years to repay, and you'd owe $14,063 in interest.

A TIMELY ISSUE

If your payment arrives by 5 p.m. of the due date, the card issuer must consider it timely, which means on time. If it's due on a weekend or holiday, you have until 5 p.m. on the next business day. But don't cut it too close.

Payment Information

Statement Balance $2,422.67
Minimum Payment Due $25.00

Minimum Payment Warning: If you make only the minimum payment each period, you will pay more in interest and it will take you longer to pay off your balance. For example:

If you make no additional charges using this card and each month you pay....	You will pay off the balance shown on this statement in about...	And you will end up paying an estimated total of...
Only the minimum payment	12 years	$4,444.00
$83.00	3 years	$2,988.00 (Savings = $1,456.00)

CHOOSING A CARD

You may decide that using just one credit card will meet your needs, but there may be times that using two would be a more economical choice. To help you decide, ask yourself:

- Do you always pay your credit card bill in full and on time each month?
- Does it sometimes take you a number of months to pay off a major purchase, such as an appliance or furniture?
- Do you regularly pay just a portion of the outstanding balance each month?

If the answer to the first question is yes, you may need just one card with a grace period. If the answer to the last question is yes, then what you want is a card with the lowest possible APR for which you qualify.

But if it sometimes takes you a little longer to pay a large bill, consider using two cards: one with a grace period that you'll pay off in full for most charges, and another, with a low APR, that you use for large purchases. In fact, you might investigate applying for a card from the retailer where you make a major purchase if you can avoid interest entirely by making all scheduled payments on time.

One caution: just never be late with these payments or the interest-free deal may evaporate and you'll be facing a hefty interest charge.

WORD TO THE WISE

Credit card issuers market their cards aggressively, often offering lower-than-average APRs, called teaser rates. They may also encourage you to transfer existing balances. You'll want to confirm what the actual rate will be when the low rate expires and the cost, if any, of balance transfers.

Using Cards

It may be hard to imagine life without credit cards, but you have to be smart about using them.

Credit cards are everywhere. But probably the smartest thing is to avoid having too many of them. The more cards you have, the more you may be tempted to spend, and the harder it may be to keep track of when the bills are due. What's more, having too much available credit may make you seem like a greater risk to new creditors.

Cards from retail stores may pose the biggest danger since not only do they tend to have higher APRs, but the stores make it so tempting to apply for and use their cards by offering discounts.

BEATING EXTRA COSTS

By paying all outstanding balances in full and on time, you can keep your credit costs under control by escaping finance charges and avoiding penalty fees.

Thanks to the Credit CARD Act of 2009, a late payment fee must be what the Federal Reserve Board calls "reasonable and proportional," which means, among other things, that it can't be more than the minimum payment that was due. The Board limits the charge for a first violation to $25 and to $35 for a second violation within six months. If you're charged more, you should complain to the issuer and then to the Consumer Financial Protection Bureau at www.consumerfinance.gov.

Further, thanks to the Act, you can't be charged an inactivity fee for not using your card. And, you can be charged an over-limit fee for spending more than your credit limit only if you agree to have the card issuer pay amounts that are over your limit. It's wiser not to.

CASH ADVANCES

Be very careful about taking cash advances with your credit card. While it may feel a lot like using a debit card, the reality is very different. Not only do you pay an upfront fee for the advance, but

interest begins to accrue immediately at a rate that's higher than your card's APR for purchases. One way to avoid this situation: simply don't choose a PIN for your credit card since you can't make cash withdrawals without one.

CARDS WITH ANNUAL FEES

Should you choose a card with an annual fee? You may not want to, as it increases the cost of using credit. It's also relatively easy to find a card with a competitive APR and no up-front charge.

The argument in favor is that some cards with annual fees may offer attractive benefits. Among these are **affinity cards** cosponsored by the issuing bank and another organization, either for-profit or nonprofit.

If you use the card regularly and charge large amounts, the card's added features, such as frequent flier miles or contributions to a nonprofit you care about, can be a plus. But you'll want to be sure that these advantages offset the added cost. They may, but they don't always. And not all affinity cards carry an annual fee.

STORING INFORMATION

Most credit cards issued by US banks store your name, the card's expiration date, your PIN and credit limit, account number, and other data in the magnetic strip on the back of the card. In most other countries, strips have been replaced with more secure computer chips encrypted with the data. Strips survive because card scanners, which are everywhere, can't read the chips. But international travelers increasingly find that their magnetic strip cards aren't accepted, potentially leaving them in a credit bind. It's something you might want to check with your issuer about if you're planning a trip.

VS.

ALTERNATE IDENTITIES

Some cards with well-known names aren't credit cards at all, but **charge cards**. You use them as you do credit cards to make purchases, but your agreement requires you to pay your bill in full each month. If you fall behind, you may be charged interest, blocked from using the card, or both. You may also find that no additional charges will be approved if you have a large outstanding balance even though you're not given a specific credit limit.

Charge cards generally have an annual fee, which can be substantial in the case of premium cards offered by particular issuers. The cost may be worth it, though, if the benefits it provides are things you would otherwise have to pay for, such as access to airline club facilities or rental car insurance if you travel a lot.

One approach is to use two cards: one a credit card and the other a charge card. That way you have access to the advantages that each may provide and are less likely to find yourself in a situation where at least one of your cards won't be honored. Occasionally a retailer will accept one type of card but not the other, which can be a serious inconvenience if you don't carry both types.

SECURITY AT A COST

If you have trouble qualifying for a credit card, you may be able to arrange for a **secured credit card** by opening a savings account and keeping a balance equal to your credit line. The account guarantees the issuer will be repaid.

However, you may find that the fees most secured cards charge reduce the actual credit you have, limiting their usefulness. And since using a secured card won't help you qualify for a conventional credit card unless the card issuer reports your use to the credit reporting agencies, you may be better off without one.

Card Rights

You're protected against excessive charges and deceptive practices.

Things can go wrong when you use credit cards. You may be a victim of scammers who make a business of ripping off other people's credit and are notoriously successful at it. You may be hounded by debt collectors for bills that you never incurred or have paid in full. And you may be frustrated by unresolved billing errors, which credit-centered legislation dating back to the Truth in Lending Act of 1968 has tried to address.

As a first step, you need to review and be sure you understand the terms of any credit arrangement you make, including the updates you're sent. Typically the agreement is in fine print and seemingly endless detail, despite the Credit CARD Act requirement that issuers provide relevant information "in plain language in plain sight."

You'll also want to keep your receipts, check them against your next statement, and notify the issuer immediately if you spot errors or find charges you don't recognize. Even if it turns out you made the purchase, it doesn't cost anything to check.

Most card issuers respond promptly if there's evidence of fraud. They usually cancel your current card and provide a new one to prevent future misuse. Many issuers are also proactive: They'll notify you if they see unusual activity, based on your normal card use. You can do your part, by letting your issuer know if you'll be traveling overseas, for example, or making an exceptionally large purchase.

MAKING CHANGES

If you find dealing with your credit issuer difficult, you can always switch to more user-friendly provider, ideally a cheaper one. Unless you've had credit problems, it should be easy to establish a new relationship. If your new rate is lower and there's no fee for a balance transfer, you may want to move your outstanding balance. Better yet, simply pay it off.

1 Never give your card number (or card) to anyone unless you are buying something or making a reservation. Since merchants can't charge your account if your check bounces, there's no reason

BE PREPARED

If you want to know more about the credit protection laws that establish your card rights, visit www.federalreserve.gov and search for "credit protection laws." What you learn can be a good defense against potential credit card problems.

LOST OR STOLEN CARDS

If your credit card is lost or stolen, and someone uses it, the Fair Credit Billing Act limits your liability to $50 if the card is used and zero if only the number is used. In fact, most card issuers don't hold you responsible for any charges. But you should notify the issuer as soon as you realize the card is missing to eliminate any questions about whether or not the charges were yours.

CANCELLING YOUR CARD

By law, you can cancel your card and avoid paying the annual fee as long as you notify the lender in writing within 40 days of receiving the bill for the fee.

PURCHASES YOU DIDN'T MAKE AND OTHER BILLING ERRORS

You have 60 days to notify the lender in writing about credit card billing errors. This includes wrong amounts of credit extended, wrong goods or services, incorrect payments or credits, computational errors, or any other disputed charges.

Card companies have 30 days to respond and up to 90 days to resolve the problem. They can't stop you from using your card while investigating the problem and can't release a bad credit report on you based on the disputed charges if you pay the rest of your bill. And if they don't respond, they can't collect the disputed amount or finance charges.

DEFECTIVE MERCHANDISE

You can legally refuse to pay for defective merchandise if it cost more than $50, and you were unable to resolve the problem with the merchant. The purchase must be made in your home state or within 100 miles of your mailing address, though companies are flexible on this matter. The price and mileage restrictions don't apply if the card issuer advertised the product or was involved in the purchase.

to write the number on your check for them. And there's no need to put your phone, name, or address on a credit card receipt. In some states, it's illegal for a retailer to ask you to do this.

2. Be careful with your receipts and billing statements. Thieves can use your number to charge purchases or even order new cards.

3. Never make your PIN available to anyone. Don't write it anywhere a thief may have access to it. It's also essential to use a PIN others can't figure out easily. But it has to be one you can remember.

Loans

You can arrange to borrow and repay the money you need for specific expenses.

When you need money to buy a car, pay college tuition, fix up your home, or anything else that requires an immediate cash outlay, you are often able to borrow the amount from a lender such as a bank or a credit union. If you know how different types of loans work and the particular features they offer, you'll be in a better position to look for the one that will be best suited for you.

In some ways, of course, all loans are alike. You borrow money, called the **principal**, and agree to pay it back over a specific **term**, or length of time, with **interest**. But the details of each individual loan can affect how much you can borrow and how much the loan will cost you.

- Whether it's an **installment** loan or a line of credit
- Whether the interest rate is **fixed** or **adjustable**
- Whether the loan is **secured** or **unsecured**

INSTALLMENT
ADJUSTABLE
FIXED
REVOLVING
SECURED

INSTALLMENT LOANS

When you take an installment loan, you borrow the money all at once and repay it in set amounts, or installments, on a regular schedule, usually once a month. Installment loans are also called closed-end loans because you must pay them off by a specific date.

SECURED LOANS

Your loan is secured when you put up **collateral**, or property, to guarantee repayment. The lender can repossess the collateral if you fail to repay. Car loans and home equity loans are the most common types of secured loans.

VS.

UNSECURED LOANS

An unsecured loan is made solely on your promise to repay. If the lender thinks you are a good risk, nothing but your signature is required. However, the lender may require a co-signer, who promises to repay if you don't. Since unsecured loans pose a bigger risk for lenders, they may have higher interest rates and stricter conditions.

CHOOSING A TERM

The term of a loan is critical to the cost of borrowing. Assuming the same principal and interest rate, you always save money with a shorter term because you pay less interest, though the monthly payments are larger. What's more, some shorter-term mortgage loans offer lower rates than longer-term loans with the same principal, reducing your cost even more. But if you're concerned about being able to afford the larger payments on a shorter-term loan, paying somewhat more interest with a longer loan may be wiser than risking the possibility of default.

Here's an example that illustrates the effect of term on three $15,000 car loans of different lengths.

LINES OF CREDIT

A personal line of credit is a type of **revolving credit**, similar in many ways to a credit card. It lets you write special checks for the amount you want to borrow, up to a limit set by the lender. The credit doesn't cost you anything until you access the line. Then you begin to pay interest on the amount you borrowed. You must repay at least a minimum amount each month plus interest, but you can repay more, or even the whole loan amount, whenever you want. Whatever you repay becomes available for you to borrow again.

Banks and credit card issuers sometimes offer lines of credit automatically to people they consider good customers. But that doesn't mean you have to borrow if you prefer not to.

for example

If you have a $10,000 line of credit, you have access to that money over and over, as long as you repay what you use:

	$ 10,000	Line of credit
–	$ 6,000	You borrow
=	$ 4,000	Available credit
+	$ 1,000	You repay
=	$ 5,000	Available credit

Advantages

- Only one application
- Instant access to credit

Disadvantages

- Potentially high interest rate
- Easy to over-borrow

FIXED RATE vs. ADJUSTABLE RATE

FIXED RATE

Many installment loans have a fixed rate. The interest rate and the monthly payments stay the same for the term of the loan.

Advantages

- Installments stay the same
- Easy to budget payments
- The cost of the loan won't increase
- No surprises

Disadvantages

- Interest remains the same, even if market rates decrease
- Initial rate higher than adjustable rate
- Not always available

ADJUSTABLE RATE

An adjustable rate loan has a variable interest rate. When the rate changes, usually every six months or once a year, the monthly payment also changes.

Advantages

- Initial rate lower than fixed rate
- Lower overall costs if rates drop
- Annual increases usually controlled
- Can be easier to qualify for

Disadvantages

- Vulnerable to rate hikes
- Hard to budget for increases
- Could cost more overall

	3 YEAR	4 YEAR	5 YEAR
Number of monthly payments	36	48	60
Amount of each payment	$456.33	$352.28	$290
Total repaid	$16,427.88	$16,909.44	$17,400
Total interest paid	**$1,427.88**	**$1,909.44**	**$2,400**

The Substance of a Loan

When you borrow, you want to know how much, for how long and at what price.

Whether you need a loan only occasionally or borrow on a more regular basis, you'll be concerned with the same basic things:

- **The amount you'll be able to borrow**
- **How long you'll have to repay**
- **What the interest charges will be**

Some loans have built-in limits. For example, if you borrow money to buy a car, the maximum you're eligible for is determined by the price of the car. If you borrow to pay tuition, there is often a per-year or four-year total that you can finance. Home equity loans are generally capped at 80% of your equity, and loans in excess of $50,000 may be more difficult to arrange.

Loans may also have built-in terms. Car loans rarely last for more than five years, in part so that the vehicle hasn't outlived its usefulness before it's paid off. Home loans tend to last 15 to 30 years.

The interest rate you pay, on the other hand, is affected by two key factors: the current rate for similar loans, which can vary widely from year to year, and your **credit score**, which is determined by how you've used credit in the past. Higher scores usually mean you are able to borrow more easily at the lowest rates currently available.

THE LOAN AGREEMENT

When you take a loan, you're committing yourself not only to repay, but to repay on a specific schedule. Those details are spelled out in the loan agreement, or **loan note**, a detailed document the lender provides. When you sign it, you've agreed to its terms and conditions. The fine print may be off-putting, but you should read it carefully. It explains exactly what you're getting—and getting into.

1. HOW MUCH CAN YOU BORROW?

2. HOW MUCH WILL IT COST?

3. WHEN DO YOU HAVE TO REPAY?

4. WHAT IF YOU DON'T PAY ON TIME?

IT ALL BEGINS WITH THE APPLICATION

Loan applications may vary, but they all ask for the same basic information:

Employment	Someone at work may be asked to verify your employment, and you may be asked to provide recent paystubs and income tax returns.
Accounts	You may be asked for your credit card account numbers and balances, for your banks' and securities firms' names, account numbers, and balances.
References	You may need business and personal associates to supply references.

I.O.U.

Contrary to popular belief, an IOU is not a binding promise to repay a loan. American legal interpretation considers it merely an acknowledgement that money is owed.

Usually you request a specific loan amount. The lender can approve it, reject it, or offer you a smaller amount. Sometimes you need to apply to more than one lender to find one that will approve your request. You may have to pay an application fee each time.

The **amount financed**, or the **principal**, is what you borrow. However, you may not actually get the entire amount that is approved. That's because the lender will usually subtract any application fees, credit-check fees, or other costs of the loan from the amount you receive. In addition, the lender may require you to use part of the loan amount to pay off another loan or to purchase insurance to cover the loan if you should die.

The cost of a loan is determined by the amount you borrow, the term, and the **annual percentage rate (APR)** that the lender offers. However, you may be able to find a loan at a better rate if you investigate what various lenders are charging before you apply.

Sometimes lenders are eager to lend, and offer lower rates or waive the fees. While you probably can't time your need to borrow to coincide with those occasions, some borrowers apply for home equity lines of credit when lenders promote them.

The loan's term is a major factor, because the longer it is, the more interest you pay. Your goal should be to borrow no more than you need, at the lowest available APR, and with the shortest **term** over which you can afford to repay.

The terms of repayment are part of your loan agreement. In most cases, you pay interest and some of the principal on a regular schedule, usually once a month.

In some cases, including some college loans, you may pay only interest for a specific period and then begin to repay the principal. In others, you pay only interest for the term of the loan and then repay the entire principal in a lump sum. Most lenders allow you to **prepay** a loan at any time. Some charge a prepayment penalty, usually about 2% of the amount borrowed, although many states prohibit this practice.

In many cases, you may have to pay a **late fee** if your payment arrives after the payment due date, and you should expect to be penalized if you send a payment check that is returned for nonsufficient funds (NSF), better known as a bounced check.

Failing to live up to the agreement is called **defaulting** on the loan. The lender may have the right to repossess and sell the property you put up as collateral.

Lenders may also impose a stiff penalty if you default. And, if they hire a collection agency or lawyer, you'll have to pay for those services, too.

Another way lenders can collect if you default is by taking, or **setting off**, the amount owed from any checking or savings account you have with the lender.

CHECK YOUR CREDIT STANDING

Before applying for a loan, it's smart to check your credit report with one of the three major credit reporting agencies—Experian, Equifax, or TransUnion—to confirm there's no negative information that you should be prepared to explain.

You can access this information for free from each agency once every 12 months at www.annualcreditreport.com or by calling 877-322-8228. In fact, it's a good idea to check your credit standing regularly, by rotating though the agencies so that you look at a different one every four months. The information isn't identical from agency to agency, but major problems will show up on all three.

If you find errors, which do occur more often than you might think, you should work to have them resolved before applying for a loan. Each site explains the procedure to follow and what your rights are if those errors are not corrected.

On Track With Credit

Your credit history affects what it costs you to borrow.

Your credit history includes the way you've used credit in the past and information in the public record. Both influence how lenders evaluate your **creditworthiness**, or how responsible they believe you will be about repaying what you borrow.

Your history is updated regularly in a **credit report** and summarized in a **credit score** by each of the three national credit reporting agencies: Experian, Equifax, and TransUnion. They make your report and score available, for a fee, to retailers, banks, insurance companies, landlords, potential employers, and others who are approved recipients and use the information to evaluate their credit risk in hiring or doing business with you.

Lenders and potential employers, in particular, go beyond your credit report and score in evaluating your applications. But—fair or not—a compromised credit report and a poor score make qualifying for credit, finding a job or an apartment, or buying insurance much harder.

A SCORE CARD

A credit score is a three-digit number calculated using a proprietary algorithm that crunches the data in your credit report. FICO scores, which range between 300 and 850, are the oldest, best known, and most frequently used. Higher scores are better. Roughly 20% of credit users have scores over 780 and another 20% below 620. The average is about 720.

There are five main factors in every FICO score:

- Payment history—basically whether you pay on time
- How much credit you're using
- How long you've been using credit
- The types of credit you use
- How much new credit you've applied for recently

Primary predictors of a below-average score are making payments more than 30 days late, having defaulted on a loan, and using more than 50% of your available credit. Several new applications for credit can also be a problem, though multiple queries for a specific type of credit within a short period—for example, a mortgage loan—generally count as a single request.

Other score providers use different formulas and sometimes a different number range. A Vantage score, for example, falls between 501 and 990.

If the score provider uses only information in your credit report, as most do, your age, income, employment history, race, ethnicity, marital status, or similar details are not factored into your score. Neither are any financial transactions that aren't credit based, including rent payments. However, bankruptcy, foreclosure, or court judgments against you that are in the public record are part of your report.

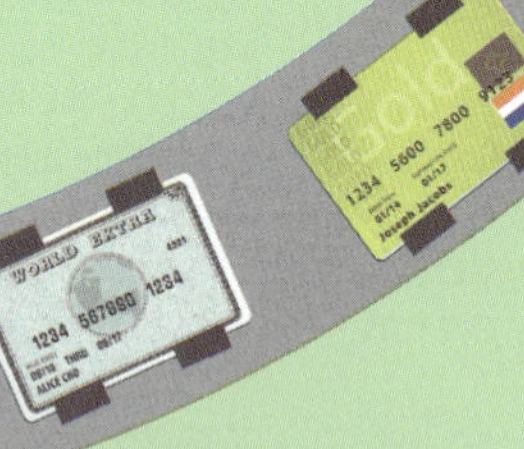

CHECK THE SCORE?

Unlike free credit reports from www.annualcreditreport.com, you generally must pay for your credit score if you want to know what it is. But there are issues, in addition to cost. For example, score providers create different versions of your score for different users by weighting the factors in their formula in different ways. In addition, scores change all the time, if usually not dramatically. And scores from different providers vary as well.

So while there may be a reason to get a ballpark sense of your FICO score before applying for a major loan, in most cases checking your credit reports regularly for problems and errors is all you need to do.

WHEN FREE ISN'T FREE
An online search for free credit reports and scores will direct you to sites that claim to provide them for free but actually don't. Many entice you to sign up for credit monitoring or other services you don't need and those without an obvious price tag want your personal data for marketing purposes.

AnnualCreditReport.com

IF YOU'RE TURNED DOWN
If your application for credit is rejected, the lender to whom you applied must give you the principal reasons for turning you down, plus provide the credit score and the name and contact information of the credit agency on whose report the score was based. You're entitled to a free copy of the report, based on the rejection, if you ask within 60 days.

If the report has an error, notify the lender right away and follow up with the credit agency following the directions on the website.

The Fair Credit Reporting Act requires the agency to investigate your claims and get back to you with its findings, although it doesn't have to correct the information if it determines it's accurate.

If the information isn't corrected, you have the right to add an explanatory comment of up to 100 words that must be included in all future reports. You can also file a complaint with the Consumer Financial Protection Bureau at www.consumerfinance.gov/complaint.

IMPROVING YOUR RECORD
If your credit history isn't as strong as you'd like it to be, you can repair it, though it may take a little time.

- Limit the number of credit cards you use, charge less, and make every credit card and loan payment on time.
- Develop and follow a plan for paying off outstanding debt, starting with debts on which you are paying the highest rates.
- Don't stop using credit, because regularly meeting your obligation to pay is key to demonstrating you're responsible.

ARE THERE ERRORS?
Based on a ten-year study, the Federal Trade Commission (FTC) reported that 26% of the people in their sample reported at least one major error in at least one of their three credit reports. Of that group, the reports of 79% were changed and 20% saw their credit scores improve enough to be offered a lower interest rate on a car loan.

Coping With Credit Problems

The key is to act before you find yourself in serious financial trouble.

Losing your job, coping with serious illness, and going through a divorce can threaten your economic security and undermine your ability to keep up with your credit obligations. So can spending more than you can comfortably afford to repay. While you may be able to juggle creditors for a time, sooner or later, you could find yourself in serious trouble.

One preventive measure is to build an emergency fund, accumulating at least six months of living expenses in readily accessible accounts. Some combination of relatively short-term certificates of deposit (CDs) and US Treasury bills will generally work. The goal is not to touch the money except in a real emergency. Ideally it will last long enough to get you back on your financial feet.

RED FLAGS

The most effective way to handle evolving credit problems is to recognize the danger signals, not ignore them:

Your debts, including your mortgage if you have one, are more than 40% of your monthly income

You're making only the minimum payment on your credit cards

You're skipping some payments entirely every month

You've borrowed up to your credit limit on one or more of your revolving credit accounts

You're using savings or investment accounts to pay your monthly bills

You're putting off essential medical or dental treatment

Unless you can increase your income or cut your expenses, you could find yourself in a situation from which it's difficult to extract yourself.

If you default, your income tax refund can be withheld to pay your debts and your wages can be garnished, which means a percentage of your paycheck is withheld to pay your creditors. It's not only embarrassing and leaves you even shorter of cash, but it could affect your job security or chances of promotion. You could also be responsible for paying court or collection costs.

THE DOCTOR IS OUT

People who call themselves credit doctors claim they can restore your credit reputation. Don't believe it, especially if they promise you won't be required to make any changes in your spending habits. Their approach is never better than quackery, and it's often fraud.

BEING PROACTIVE

If you owe more than you can repay, ask your creditors to change the terms of your credit agreements. They may agree to add the amount you are behind to the end of a loan, reduce your monthly payment, or both. This approach will extend the repayment period and cost you more in finance charges, but it may keep you from drowning in debt.

And don't wait too long to act. In many cases, including most mortgage loans and student loans, it's only possible to work out repayment if you have not defaulted. Information about possible remedies for repaying federal student loans is available at www.studentaid.ed.gov. For mortgage issues, begin by checking with your lender or loan servicer. The servicer is the bank or other organization to which you make payments.

You may want to seek professional help from an accredited credit counselor who can help create a payment plan. You need to be careful in selecting someone to work with, as qualifications vary. Before you choose, be sure you know the kinds of advice the counselor will provide and what the service will cost. You may want to search online to see if any complaints or other problems emerge when you type in a prospective counselor's name or agency affiliation.

You can also check with the National Foundation for Credit Counseling (www.nfcc.org) or the Association of Independent Consumer Credit Counseling Agencies (www.aiccca.org) for a referral in your area.

ONE LOAN FROM MANY

In some cases, you may want to investigate **loan consolidation**. In that case, you take a new loan large enough to pay off your existing debt, so that you owe just one lender rather than many. But unless you can confirm that the cost of the new loan will be less than the combined costs of your existing loans, you may be facing greater hardship.

The interest rates and fees on consolidated loans tend to be high, especially since you already have damaged credit. And some loan consolidators impose a large prepayment penalty if you want to pay off the debt early.

The one place consolidation may make the most sense, and is apt to be reasonable, is with federal student loans that you take directly from the government.

WHAT ABOUT BANKRUPTCY?

Bankruptcy is the last resort for resolving credit problems, a harsh but legal remedy for preventing financial disaster. In general, bankruptcy is a three-step process:

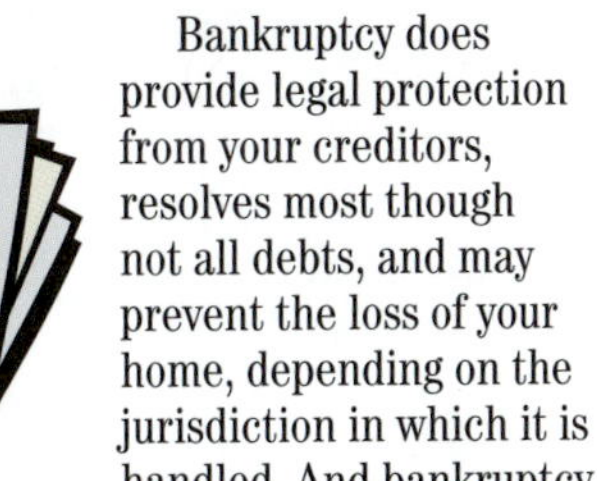

1. You file a petition in federal or state court saying that you are **insolvent**, which means you have no assets to pay your debts.
2. You work out a **repayment plan** with your creditors and the court.

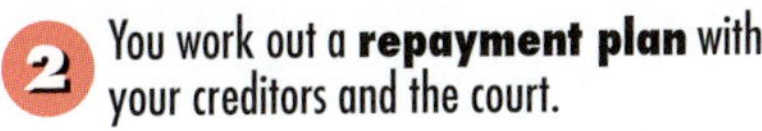

3. You **discharge your debts**, or settle them, typically for less than the full value of what you owe.

Bankruptcy does provide legal protection from your creditors, resolves most though not all debts, and may prevent the loss of your home, depending on the jurisdiction in which it is handled. And bankruptcy does offer you the chance to start again.

On the other hand, your financial affairs are public knowledge, hashed out in court and part of the public record. Your credit standing is seriously damaged, you forfeit assets, and some debts still remain outstanding.

It's essential—and in some cases mandatory—to consult an experienced attorney before filing for bankruptcy.

Buying a Home

To buy or not to buy? It may be more complicated than you think.

Is now the right time to buy a home instead of renting? Should you sell the home you're living in and buy another one? The answers to these questions are always a combination of financial and personal priorities, sometimes prompted by a new job or a growing family.

A BUYER'S CHECKLIST

If you're thinking seriously about buying, you'll want to:

- ✓ Evaluate how much you have for a down payment, either from savings or potential profit from the sale of your current home
- ✓ Estimate what you can afford to spend by reviewing your budget, consulting with your financial advisers, and comparing the results of several online home-buying calculators—though the calculators may ask for information you don't have, such as estimated real estate taxes and insurance costs
- ✓ Start looking at homes in your price range in areas you have identified as places you'd like to live

Unless you qualify for a Federal Housing Administration (FHA) mortgage, a Department of Veterans Affairs home loan guarantee, assistance through the Community Reinvestment Act (CRA), or another government program—including people buying in rural areas and people with disabilities—you should expect lenders to require a 20% cash down payment.

When estimating what you can afford, remember that you have to include real estate taxes, which can vary dramatically from place to place. If you have children, remember that higher real estate taxes may be correlated with a good public school system. So paying higher taxes may be cheaper in the long run than paying for private school. The same is true about proximity to public transportation if you

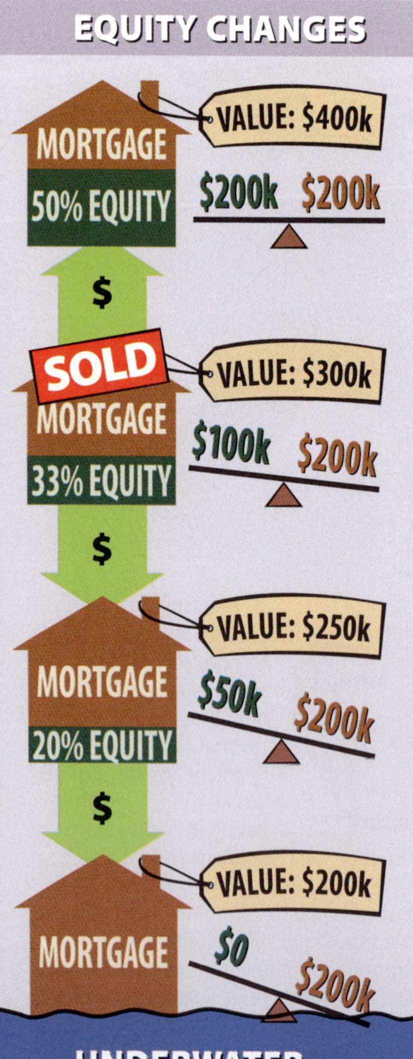

IT'S ALL ABOUT EQUITY

When you make a down payment on a home, that amount determines your equity, or the percentage of the property you actually own. The more you put down, the greater your equity. And, as you pay off the mortgage loan principal, your equity increases. When the loan is fully paid, your equity is 100%, and the home is yours, free and clear.

But there is another factor at work in building equity: the market value of real estate, which changes all the time. That means your equity can increase if the market value of your home increases. But, the reverse is also true. If the market value drops, your equity could shrink, a situation that a large number of homeowners faced during the fiscal crisis starting in 2008.

In a simplified example, assume that a home you bought for $300,000 with a $200,000 mortgage grew in value to $400,000. Your initial equity of 33%

commute. The catch is that good schools and good transportation don't necessarily go hand-in-hand.

In the final analysis, flexibility is key to finding a home that meets your financial and personal needs. So is waiting for the right opportunity.

THE BUYING PROCESS

Most homebuyers pay part of a home's purchase price, called the **down payment**, in cash, and use a **mortgage loan** from a bank, credit union, mortgage banker, or other lender to close, or finalize, the purchase.

At least six months before you expect to apply for a mortgage loan, you should check your **credit report** using www.annualcreditreport.com to be sure there are no potential credit problems that might make it harder for a lender to approve your application. If you find a major error that could hurt your creditworthiness, try to have it resolved by following the directions on the credit reporting agency website.

Then shop around for the lowest **annual percentage rate (APR)** being offered for loan term you want. If you already have an account with a potential lender, you'll want to start there, asking if you would be eligible for a preferred rate.

ASKING FIRST

The customary approach to applying for a mortgage is to wait until you find the home you want to buy and then look for a lender. But you may want to investigate **preapproval**. This means you apply for a mortgage loan before you have chosen a property. The lender will let you know whether or not you're approved and how much you'll be able to borrow.

Preapproval is often a good idea since you can shop with more confidence when you know how much you can afford to spend. Preapproval can also make you a more attractive buyer, as the seller can be confident that you can get a loan. But there are fees involved, as there are with any loan application, so you don't want to take this step until you're serious about buying.

PRE-APPROVED

Another approach is to seek **prequalification**. In this case, a mortgage lender confirms that you will probably be approved and for how much but does not make a commitment to lend.

(your \$100,000 divided by the \$300,000 value) would increase to 50% (your \$100,000 plus the \$100,000 divided by \$400,000). That is, you'd owe around \$200,000 on a home worth \$400,000.

But, if the home's market value decreased to \$250,000, your equity would shrink to 20% if you still owed \$200,000. And the value dropped below \$200,000, as it could in a serious market downturn, your equity would drop to 0% and you would actually owe more than the home was worth. That's known as being underwater.

While real estate values don't change overnight, you don't pay off a loan's principal that quickly either. In fact, it takes more than 20 years of a 30-year loan to pay off even half the principal.

The prospect of price changes in the housing market shouldn't drive you away from buying. The changes often work in your favor. But the potential for a loss in value is worth considering.

Making an Offer

There are often twists and turns, and even some bumps, on the road to buying a home.

Home prices are negotiable, but the bargaining power you have—or would like to have—depends on the level of activity in the real estate market, the number of homes available in your price range, and sometimes on how eager the seller is to make a deal.

In a strong real estate market, or one where homes sell almost as quickly as they are available for sale, the person who ends up acquiring the property is often the one who offers the price the seller is asking, or sometimes a higher amount. In a slow market, in contrast, the successful bid may offer significantly less than the asking price.

One way to be in tune with the market is to work with an experienced real estate professional who is sensitive to the type of property you are looking for and the housing prices in different communities within the region. You can also do some checking on your own, by noting how long "For Sale" signs are posted and how many houses are for sale, as well by tracking real estate websites.

HOW THE PROCESS WORKS

In general, a home is **listed**, or put up for sale, at the best price the seller thinks someone will pay, given current market conditions. There's no official pricing—and very similar houses may be listed at different prices. Some sellers consult several real estate professionals and agree to list with the one who suggests the highest price.

Most homes are listed with the local Multiple Listing System (MLS), which means that any licensed real estate professional—not only the listing broker—can show the home to prospective buyers and negotiate the sale. A small number of sellers offer their property directly to buyers.

Brokers and other real estate representatives are typically paid a percentage of the sales price for negotiating the sale of a listed home. If the professional who sells the home works for a different firm than the listing broker—which is often the case—the two firms share the commission.

In fact, you don't pay the selling broker's fee. The seller does, though the purchase price reflects that cost. Some buyers hire a buyer's agent to represent them in the transaction. That agent's fee may be a percentage of the listing broker's fee or be paid separately by the buyer.

MAKING AN OFFER

When you find a home you'd like, you tell your agent you want to make a **bid**, or price offer. Unless the owner is selling without a broker, you don't make the offer directly. If there are negotiations and several rounds of offers, all of them are handled through your agent.

Like housing prices themselves, offer prices reflect the market. In a strong market, you risk losing out entirely if you make an offer significantly lower than the asking price. What you don't want to do in the excitement of negotiation is to bid more than you can comfortably afford to pay or than you believe the property is really worth. On the other hand, if real estate is moving slowly—which can happen for many reasons—you may be able to negotiate significant savings by opening with a very low bid.

To come close to the market price, or what the house will actually sell for—in contrast to the asking price that the seller would like to get—you can check the history of comparable homes that have sold recently in the same neighborhood. You can also find out when the seller bought the home and what it cost at that time. That information is available in local government offices and sometimes on real estate websites.

You may also try to evaluate how eager the seller is to get rid of the property. For example, some sellers may have already purchased another home or are moving out of the area and are eager to close a deal. The same is true if the home has been on the market for a longer-than-average time, and the sellers are getting anxious about finding a buyer. The sellers may also be settling an estate and want to conclude a sale quickly.

COMING TO TERMS

If your bid is accepted, you normally make a small payment, often in the $1,000 range, to secure your commitment. The amount—and what this payment is called—vary from place to place around the country. In some areas, it's called a **binder**, in others a **good-will payment**, and in still others, **earnest money**.

In most cases, the amount is applied to the initial cash payment you owe if you sign a contract. If the deal falls through, you often—but not always—get the money back. It's a good idea to ask before you make a payment.

LOOKING FOR PROBLEMS

Once your offer is accepted, you should arrange for a licensed building inspector to evaluate the property. Your lender or real estate agent may recommend a firm or independent contractor, or you can check local listings.

The inspector's job is to uncover any serious structural or maintenance problems that could require expensive repairs. If there are cracks in the foundation, water damage, substandard electrical wiring, or a leaky roof, you may want to reduce your offer or withdraw it altogether.

You'll pay a fixed fee for the inspection, typically several hundred dollars. But you're likely to get your money's worth, especially if anything needs work, since evidence from the report may help you negotiate a lower price for the home.

Signing a Sales Contract

The terms of a purchase are spelled out in a legal contract the buyer and seller sign.

GETTING EXPERT ADVICE

It's important that you hire an experienced real estate attorney to review the sales contract before you sign. The document's language is specialized, and may include some conditions that favor the seller rather than you. You don't want to agree to anything that could cost you extra time or money, or that might limit your rights.

You may want to ask your financial adviser, real estate agent, or lender to recommend a real estate attorney. Or if you've worked with an attorney in a different capacity, you may want to ask him or her for a recommendation.

An attorney may charge an hourly rate or a set fee calculated as a percentage of the purchase price. Generally, one or the other approach is standard in the area where you're looking, and the amount may not be negotiable. You may also have to pay for the services of your financing provider's attorney, again depending on local custom. Using the provider's attorney may be a cost-saving alternative, but hiring your own legal representative is a better idea and worth the added cost.

DIFFERING VALUES

The **market value** of a property is the amount you're willing to pay to buy it. The **appraised value**, on the other hand, is what a real estate appraiser working for a lender believes it is worth, based on comparable houses in the community and his or her judgment and experience.

The appraised value determines the size of the mortgage loan a lender will provide. If it's less than you need to buy the home, you may need to increase your down payment, find another lender, or change your plans.

THE SELLER'S AGENT & ATTORNEY

FINALIZING THE CONTRACT

When representatives for you and the seller have agreed to the terms of the contract, you both sign the document. You typically make a cash down payment to the seller's agent, which is held in reserve in an **escrow account** until the sale is finalized. The amount of the required payment is stated in the contract, and varies based on local custom. The maximum is rarely more than 10% of the purchase price and may be less. The balance of the down payment is due at the closing.

If the sale falls through, you may or may not get the deposit back, depending on whether or not there is a contingency clause to this effect in the contract. Unless a contingency is standard practice, such as one voiding the contract if the buyer can't find a mortgage, one or the other party may not be willing to agree to including it.

There's no way to predict how long contract negotiations may take. They can move along briskly, but they can also be stalled if you, the seller, or your representatives can't agree on all the details. And since there are a number of people involved—the seller, the seller's agent, the seller's attorney, you, your agent, and your attorney—making even minor changes to the agreement and getting them approved can take time. One risk you face is that until the contract is signed, the seller may receive a higher offer and reject yours.

The period before you sign is probably the last opportunity you'll have to revise your offer if the inspection has turned up any problems with the home. This means you'll want to have the report in your hands before the contract discussions end.

NEGOTIATION UNDERWAY

Sellers may be willing to accept a reduced price or to hold part of the mortgage if you're unable to borrow the full amount, especially if they're eager to sell. Real estate brokers may agree to a reduced commission if a sale is stalled over price, especially if a representative from the listing firm is handling the transaction.

SETTING THE RULES

Buyers or sellers can add contingencies, or conditions, to a real estate contract that must be met if the agreement is to be finalized. Buyers may demand that certain repairs or improvements be made. Sellers may want the right to sell to another bidder after a specific date if financing is not final.

FREE AND CLEAR TITLE

You, as the buyer, must be able to obtain a **free and clear title** to the property. The title provides assurance that no other person, organization, or government has any legal or financial claim that would limit ownership rights. Without this title, you take the risk of losing the money invested in the property should there ever be a court-imposed settlement requiring the new owner to make good on a claim.

To obtain this title, you pay a title company or title attorney to examine the public record for any outstanding claims against the property and provide title insurance to protect your lender's interest in the property. You can also protect your equity by buying owner's coverage for an extra charge.

Qualifying for a Mortgage

Being able to buy a home usually depends on being able to borrow.

Lenders evaluate, or underwrite, your mortgage application to decide if you're a good risk. In general, what they want to see is:

- A down payment, or initial cash payment, of 20% or more of the purchase price
- No more than 28% of your gross annual income needed to pay PITI—principal, interest, homeowners insurance, and property taxes
- A strong credit report, without late payments or defaults
- A debt-to-income (DTI) ratio of no more than 43%, which means that you need no more than 43% of your gross annual income to pay your mortgage plus your other debts
- A history of regular employment at a full-time job

MEETING LENDER STANDARDS

You may hear the criteria that lenders use in evaluating your application for a mortgage loan described as the big three.

Capacity addresses your ability to have enough cash for the down payment and closing costs, keep up with the loan payments, and still have some assets in reserve. In general, capacity depends on your current monthly income, your investment assets, and your other financial obligations.

Collateral is the value of the property that you plan to buy. A lender requires that it be worth at least as much as you're borrowing to buy it. To make that judgment, the lender hires a professional appraiser to evaluate the property both on its own merits and in relation to comparable properties.

Creditworthiness depends on how you have used credit in the past, including loans and lines of credit. Lenders use both a credit report and a credit score based on the report to make this assessment.

Some lenders may use information on your rent and utility payments and other contractual spending to evaluate the risk you pose. This is known as alternative documentation. They may also use automated underwriting systems, which are software programs that use

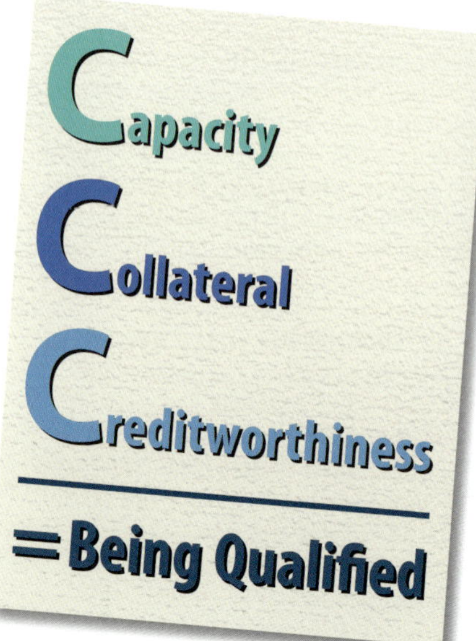

OTHER ROUTES TO OWNERSHIP

There are other ways to buy. You may want to investigate a rent-to-own arrangement or consider buying at auction.

When you rent-to-own, you sign a contract with the owner that gives you an option to buy, with some or all of your lease payments being credited toward the agreed-upon sale price. There are potentially some drawbacks, though, including the possibility the sellers will change their minds if real estate prices go up, so be sure to have an experienced local real estate lawyer review the contract before you sign.

Auctions, where you can buy homes that have been repossessed or are being sold to settle an estate, can help you find a great house at a great price. But there are serious risks for inexperienced buyers. Unless you're serious about becoming an auction expert, you may do better looking for short sales—homes that are being sold below value so that the sellers can pay off their loans at a price their lenders have agreed to accept.

statistics from comparable purchases by comparable buyers to provide an objective measurement of the risk of approving your application.

IF YOU'RE TURNED DOWN

If your application is turned down, there are a number of steps you can take.

- You might apply to a different lender, as loan criteria vary among lenders
- You might look for a less expensive home that will still meet your needs
- You might work with a mortgage broker to find a lender, though there will be a fee

REVISED RULES

The Consumer Financial Protection Bureau (CFPB), acting on the changes mandated by Congress in the Dodd-Frank Act, prohibits qualified mortgages from including negative amortization provisions, interest-only payments, balloon payments, terms longer than 30 years, or points and fees in excess of 3% of the loan amount—though third-party costs, including title insurance, taxes, and filing fees are exempt from the 3% rule. Negative amortization occurs when interest you haven't paid is added to your outstanding principal.

There are exceptions, including those for mortgages in rural areas. And different rules apply to subprime loans, which have higher-than-market APRs. But if you have questions about the terms of a mortgage you're offered, consult your lawyer and contact the CFPB at www.consumerfinance.gov.

THE WAITING GAME

Within three days of applying for a mortgage loan you should be mailed a **good faith estimate (GFE)** of what the closing, or settlement, fees will cost you if you use that lender. In addition, you'll receive a **Truth in Lending (TIL)** form that states the APR and other details about your costs.

You may want to apply to two or perhaps three lenders and use the GFE and TIL forms they provide to compare the offers and potentially negotiate a lower rate or lower fees. Remember, though, that these numbers are estimates, and they could change somewhat by the actual closing.

It can take up to 30 days after you've submitted a completed application to get an answer from a lender, though the wait may be shorter. If you're approved, you'll get a written commitment letter stating the terms of the loan agreement and how long you have to set a closing date.

If your application is successful, you should try to lock in the interest rate that's available at the time it's approved, with the understanding that if rates drop you'll actually finalize the purchase at the lower rate. Some lenders charge a fee for a lock-in, which you can ask about when you do your initial research.

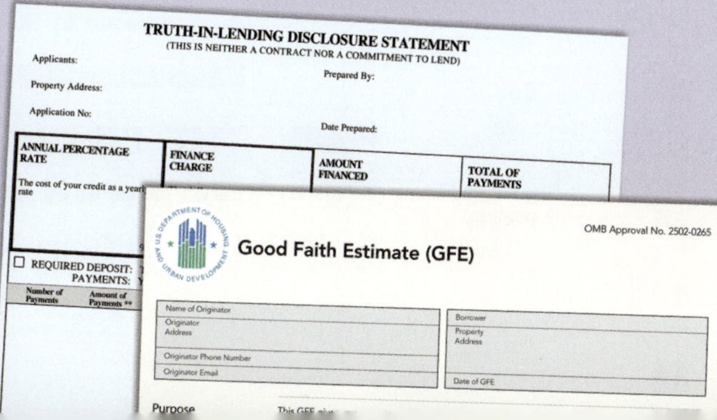

TRUTH-IN-LENDING DISCLOSURE STATEMENT
(THIS IS NEITHER A CONTRACT NOR A COMMITMENT TO LEND)

Applicants:
Property Address:
Application No:
Prepared By:
Date Prepared:

ANNUAL PERCENTAGE RATE	FINANCE CHARGE	AMOUNT FINANCED	TOTAL OF PAYMENTS
The cost of your credit as a yearl rate			

☐ REQUIRED DEPOSIT:
PAYMENTS:

Number of Payments	Amount of Payments **

Good Faith Estimate (GFE)
OMB Approval No. 2502-0265

Name of Originator
Originator Address
Originator Phone Number
Originator Email
Borrower
Property Address
Date of GFE
Purpose

The Cost of a Mortgage

The cost of a mortgage depends on the amount you borrow, the APR, and how long you take to repay.

Since monthly payments spread the cost of a mortgage over a long period of time, it's easy to forget the total expense. For example, if you borrow $200,000 for 30 years at 6% interest, your total repayment will be around $431,680, more than two and a half times the original loan.

What seems like minor differences in the interest rate can add up to a lot of money over 30 years. At 7% the total repaid would be $479,160, about $47,480 more than at the 6% rate.

TERM (LENGTH OF THE LOAN)
The longer the term, the lower the monthly payments, but the more you'll pay in total.

RATE
Over time, a lower interest rate will have the greatest impact on overall cost.

LOAN AMOUNT (PRINCIPAL)

The amount you borrow. This is the amount plus interest that you must repay over the term of the loan.

\+ **INTEREST**

Interest is the percentage of principal you pay to borrow. It's the primary component of the APR, and is determined in large part by the current cost of borrowing in the economy and your creditworthiness.

\+ **POINTS (PREPAID INTEREST)**

Interest that you prepay at the closing. Each point is 1% of the loan amount. For example, on a $90,000 loan with two points, you'd prepay $1,800.

\+ **FEES**

Fees include application fees, loan origination fees, and other initial costs imposed by the lender.

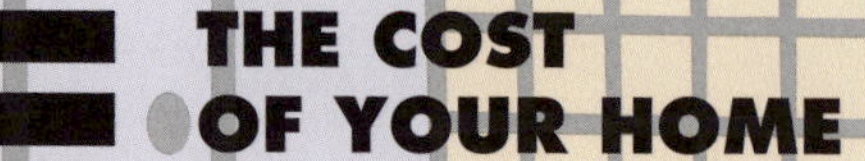

= **THE COST OF YOUR HOME**

Bottom line: Any of the factors will increase the overall cost, but a higher interest rate and longer term will have the greatest impact.

PAYING OFF YOUR LOAN

You repay a mortgage loan in a series of monthly installments over the term, a process known as **amortization**. Over the first few years, most of each payment is allocated to interest and only a small portion to paying off the principal. By year 20 of a 30-year mortgage, the amounts allocated to each equal out. And, by the last few years, you're paying mostly principal and very little interest.

CUTTING MORTGAGE EXPENSES

The amount you borrow, the finance charges—which combine interest and fees—and the time it takes you to repay are the factors that make buying a home expensive. So finding a way to reduce one or more of them can save you money.

1 **Make a larger down payment.** The less you borrow, the less interest you'll pay. Since the interest is calculated on a smaller base, your payments will be lower. And if your down payment is at least 20% of the purchase price, you won't be required to purchase private mortgage insurance (PMI), which adds to your borrowing costs.

The primary drawback to a larger down payment may be cutting too deeply into your savings, making it difficult to cover other expenses.

2 **Consider a shorter loan.** With a shorter term, you pay less interest overall on the same principal. You may also qualify for a somewhat lower APR, which would reduce your total cost even more. But your monthly payments are higher than if you choose a longer term. So you run the risk of committing yourself to larger payments than you can afford.

3 **Make more payments.** You can pay more than the amount required by your contract, either by making more payments or paying an extra amount with each regular payment. If you do the latter, be sure to make it clear that the extra amount should be used to reduce principal, not prepay interest. Lenders may offer a bi-weekly payment plan, but managing the extra payments yourself gives you more flexibility and may reduce the loan faster.

However, you might earn more by investing the money than you would save by paying off the principal faster, particularly since you'd still end up paying most of the interest.

THE EFFECT OF THE TERM ON A $100,000 MORTGAGE

	Monthly amount at different interest rates			
Term	**6%**	**6.5%**	**7%**	**7.5%**
15-year	$1,688	$1,742	$1,798	$1,854
30-year	$600	$632	$665	$699
	Total payment			
Term	**6%**	**6.5%**	**7%**	**7.5%**
15-year	$303,840	$313,560	$323,640	$333,720
30-year	$431,640	$455,040	$479,160	$503,280

A POINT WELL TAKEN

Lenders might be willing to raise a loan's interest rate by a fraction (say ⅛% or ¼%) and lower the number of points—or the reverse—as long as they make the same profit. The advantages of fewer points are lower closing costs and laying out less money when you're apt to need it most. But if you plan to keep the house longer than five to seven years, paying more points to get a lower interest rate will reduce your long-term cost.

OTHER COSTS OF OWNING

Principal and interest are major components of the cost of buying a home, but they aren't the only ones. You'll also owe real estate taxes, which can vary dramatically from state to state and from region to region within a state.

The taxes, which are based on the **assessed value** of your property and the municipality's tax rate, typically pay for public schools, police and fire protection, highways, and a raft of other government services. Assessed value, which is determined by an assessor working for a particular municipality, usually differs, at least to some extent, from both the market value and the appraised value.

There is also the cost of homeowners insurance, which your lender will require to protect its investment and which you should have to protect your equity. You may also be required to have flood insurance, which is separate.

In most cases, your monthly mortgage payment includes all four costs, typically shortened to PITI, for principal, interest, taxes, and insurance.

Mortgage Rates

Mortgages can have either fixed or adjustable rates, or sometimes a combination of the two.

The interest you owe on a mortgage loan may be calculated just once or adjusted many times. With a fixed-rate loan, the total you'll owe is determined at closing. With an adjustable-rate loan (ARM), the amount changes as the cost of borrowing changes.

Fixed-Rate Mortgages

Fixed-rate or **conventional** mortgages have been around since the 1930s. The total interest and monthly payments are set at the closing. You repay the principal and interest in equal, usually monthly, installments over a 15-, 20- or 30-year period. You know from the start what you'll pay and for how long.

In most cases, you can renegotiate the loan to get a lower rate if borrowing costs drop. If you sell your home, you can pay off your loan early, though there may be a prepayment penalty.

PLUSES

- You always know your loan costs, so you can plan your budget more easily
- Your mortgage won't increase if interest rates go up

MINUSES

- Initial rates and closing costs are higher than for ARMs
- Your monthly payments may be larger than with ARMs
- You won't benefit if interest rates drop, but have to re-finance to get the lower rates

HYBRID MORTGAGES

Choosing between a fixed-rate or an adjustable-rate mortgage isn't an all-or-nothing proposition. In fact, there are hybrids that offer certain advantages of each type while softening some of their drawbacks.

Among the most popular are mortgages that offer an initial fixed rate for a specific period, usually five, seven, or ten years, and then are adjusted. The adjustment may be a one-time change, to whatever the current rate is. More typically, the rate changes regularly over the balance of the loan term, usually once a year.

One appeal of the **multiyear mortgage**, as these hybrids are often called, is that the borrower can get a lower rate on the fixed-term portion of the mortgage than if the rate were set for the entire 30 years. That's because the lender isn't limited by a long-term agreement to a rate that may turn out to be unprofitable.

The lower rate also means it's easier to qualify for a mortgage, since the monthly payment will be lower. That's a real plus, especially if you're a first-time buyer.

For people who plan to move within a few years, especially if it's within the period during which they're paying the fixed rate, there's the added appeal of paying less now and not having to worry about what might happen when the adjustable period begins. In fact, the typical mortgage lasts only about seven years. Then the borrower moves or refinances and pays off the balance.

TEASER RATES

The introductory rate you pay for the first months of an adjustable-rate mortgage is almost always lower than the actual cost of borrowing the money. What it means for the borrower is not only a few months of relief but also lower closing costs. The effect is to make mortgages more accessible to more people.

What it means for the lender is being able to adjust the rate upward when the introductory period ends, while staying competitive with other lenders.

However, in evaluating whether you'll be able to afford the mortgage, the lender must calculate your monthly payment at the highest amount it could possibly be within the first five years of the term, not what that amount would be at closing.

Adjustable-Rate Mortgages

ARMs were introduced in the 1980s to help more buyers qualify for mortgages, and to protect lenders by letting them pass along higher interest costs to borrowers.

HOW ARMs WORK

An ARM has a variable interest rate: The rate changes on a regular schedule—such as once a year—to reflect fluctuations in the cost of borrowing. Unlike fixed-rate mortgages, the total cost can't be figured in advance, and monthly payments may rise or fall over the term of the loan.

Lenders determine the new rate using two measures:

- **An index**, which must be a published figure, like the rate on one-year US Treasury securities or the cost-of-funds indexes. Be sure to check the index. Some fluctuate more—and change more rapidly—than others
- **The margin**, a predetermined percentage, such as 1.5%, which is added to the index to determine the new rate

PLUSES

- Low initial rates (sometimes called **teaser rates**) reduce your closing costs and early monthly payments
- Your interest rate will drop if interest rates go down

MINUSES

- It's hard to budget housing costs, since monthly payments can change at adjustment
- Interest costs rise after the teaser rate expires
- You may have to pay more interest if rates go up

CAPPED COSTS

All ARMs have **caps**, or limits, on the amount the interest rate can change. An **annual cap** limits the rate change each year, usually to two percentage points, while a **lifetime cap** limits the change over the life of the loan, typically to five or six points.

Be careful: Lifetime caps are based on the actual cost and not on the introductory rate. For example, with a 4% teaser rate and a 6.5% actual interest cost, your rate could go as high as 12.5% with a six-point lifetime cap.

A WORD OF WARNING

The size of your down payment, your employment history and earnings record, your credit score, and the amount you want to borrow all affect the interest rate you're offered. If that rate is higher than the rate the lender is advertising, ask for an explanation. If you're not convinced, you may want to apply to a different lender or complain to the Consumer Financial Protection Bureau (www.consumerfinance.gov) if you suspect discrimination.

The Closing

Before you can open the door to your new home, you must close the transaction.

When you've chosen a home, your financing is in place, and the paperwork is done, only the **closing**—sometimes called the **settlement**—remains before you get the keys to your new home. This process varies from state to state and sometimes even within the same state, following local tradition.

THEMES AND VARIATIONS

A closing is typically a meeting of all the parties involved in the transaction, or their representatives. This includes you, your lender, the real estate agent, your attorney, the seller, the seller's attorney, representatives from the title company and the survey company, and perhaps others.

During the meeting, which may be run by the attorney for your lender or by a settlement agent, you and the seller sign the documents that legalize the transfer of the property, the seller is paid, and you write checks to cover all the remaining charges.

The process is different when settlement is handled by an escrow agent. Then there isn't a gathering of the interested parties. Representatives for the buyer and seller sign the required papers, hand over the checks, and mail the documents to you when the transaction is completed.

A STATEMENT OF FACT

There's an official document, HUD-1, that's called the **closing statement** or **settlement statement**. It itemizes all the fees and expenses you pay at the closing that were included in the **good faith estimate (GFE)** that you received from your lender. You can find sample copies of these forms using the search bar on the Department of Housing and Urban Development (HUD) website at www.hud.gov. You can also download a copy of *Shopping for Your Home Loan*, HUD's Settlement Costs Booklet. It's a valuable resource.

You have the right to see the statement one business day before the closing, and you should check it to be certain there are no errors or unexpected costs. (There is an exception when an escrow agent handles the closing. In that case, you don't have the right to see the statement in advance.)

THE MONEY TRAIL

When closing is over, you begin to make your monthly mortgage payments. It probably will feel a lot like paying rent. But it's different: You're buying something of value with each payment.

Basically what happens is that you mail a check or, more frequently, arrange an electronic transfer of money from your account to the account your lender has designated to receive the payment. At least once a year, and sometimes more often, you'll get an account statement detailing what you've paid and where you stand in building your equity. Your tax-deductible interest payments will be listed separately. You should save these statements as part of your permanent record.

PREPAYING THE BILLS

You may be billed separately to cover real estate taxes and insurance, or those amounts may be itemized on your payment invoice each month. Typically, you make the first payment toward these expenses at the closing and a little more than one-twelfth of your annual total with each of your monthly payments. This process guarantees there'll be money available as the bills come due.

These prepayments may go into an escrow or impound account—basically, a parking place—from which your payments are withdrawn. In many states, the law requires that escrow accounts pay interest, though the rate is typically low. State laws may also require that at least one month a year your escrow account should hold no more than one-sixth of your total tax and insurance bills. Typically, it's the month following the month your largest bill is paid.

PAYING YOUR SHARE

You typically split some of the annual costs of owning the home with the seller. For example, suppose you buy a home on June 1, and the seller has paid school taxes for the year on December 1. The seller would absorb six months of the tax bill—the length of time spent in the house that tax year—and you would reimburse him or her for the other six months, when you'll be living in the house. In this case, if the tax was $2,500, you'd owe the seller $1,250.

AT YOUR SERVICE

In many cases, the lender who provides your financing continues to collect your payments as long as you live in your home. But sometimes the contract is sold to another provider. If that happens, the terms of your agreement don't change, but the address to which you send your payment does, and so do the people you deal with if questions arise.

When you sign your initial financing agreement you must be told whether your contract can be sold and what your provider's past practice has been. Some providers routinely sell and others don't.

If your contract is sold, the bank or other financial services company that collects your payments is known as the **servicer** of the loan. This firm keeps records of your payments, recalculates payments due on ARMs as required, and reports information on your tax-deductible expenditures to you and the Internal Revenue Service (IRS) using IRS Form 1098.

WHAT CLOSING COSTS COST

On average, closing costs are 2% to 3% of the amount you're borrowing, though they could be 6% or more in areas where property taxes, state transfer fees, or both, are high. Since these costs must be paid in cash, you need to anticipate them in calculating what you can afford to spend on a home.

Owning a Home

A home can be both a big responsibility and an enormous satisfaction.

When you buy a home, you're making a personal as well as a financial investment. It's your job to maintain your home so that you'll be comfortable living there. And repairs and improvements that are a landlord's responsibility when you rent are yours when you own. Equally important, you must live up to the financial terms of your mortgage loan, which always requires you to make your monthly payments in full and on time.

KEEPING UP TO DATE

If you fall behind on your payments, you run the risk of **foreclosure**. That means the finance provider has the right to repossess the property and sell it to recover amounts that are still due. If that happens, you may lose all the money you've invested, and you will be without a place to live.

The key is not to wait if you find yourself having trouble making payments. As soon as you realize you may fall behind, you should arrange a meeting with your lender or loan servicer to explore your options.

You may be reassured to know that foreclosure isn't attractive to financing providers either. It takes time and costs money. Most would much rather work with you to stretch out your payment schedule or find some other way for you to meet your obligations. But you shouldn't begin to make partial, or reduced, payments until your contract has been officially changed to reflect the new terms. Unauthorized partial payments could be rejected, putting you in **default**.

You can seek advice from a HUD-certified mortgage counselor whose advice may help you find a workable solution. You can find more information at www.hud.gov. You should also contact the NeighborhoodWorks organization at www.nw.org.

AN ANNUAL CHECK-UP FOR A HEALTHY HOME

At least once a year you should check the major mechanical and structural areas of your home, including the heating and air conditioning systems, the plumbing, roofing, gutters, doors, windows, and stairs. Keep in mind that it's easier to fix a problem when it's small. If you wait, repairs generally cost significantly more.

Do It Yourself

If you're not confident of your ability to detect potential problems, you can hire a professional to do the initial check-up. Or, you might refer to the inspection report you received when you bought your home for a list of the items the inspector looked at. And you should start identifying a list of repair experts. Sooner or later you're likely to need a plumber, an electrician, and an appliance-repair company.

Contractor

TAKING ON BIGGER JOBS

If you want to make major repairs, or renovate or remodel your home, you'll need to find experienced, reliable contractors by asking family, friends, and neighbors for recommendations. Be sure to ask about the kind of work they hired the contractors to do, and how happy they were with the results.

Once you've got a short list of contractors, ask each one to submit a **bid**. A bid is a legal offer to do a job for a specific amount of money. The bids should be very detailed, including the materials the contractor plans to use, a timeline for when it will be completed, and how the clean-up will be handled.

As you evaluate the bids, weigh quality against cost. The lowest bid, though attractive, might rely on low-quality materials or might rush the job in order to cut costs. You should also consider how you feel about each of the candidates before you make a final decision. Remember that you have to work with your contractor on a daily basis. You want someone you're comfortable with and who seems interested in doing the job.

HOMEBUYER BEWARE

It's always a good idea to make sure any contractor you hire is licensed, has insurance, and carries industry-recognized credentials. Both the National Association of Home Builders (www.nahb.org) and The National Association of the Remodeling Industry (www.nari.org) have listings of member contractors on their websites. You can also check with your community leaders or the local Better Business Bureau if you don't have personal recommendations.

And always be on your guard for unscrupulous people who take advantage of homeowners, particularly those who may be uncertain about what work should be done. These people often use scare tactics to convince you to hire them for any number of jobs from paving driveways to replacing windows to whatever they think of next.

USEFUL INFORMATION

If you've just bought your first home, you might want to download a copy of IRS Publication 530, "Tax Information for First-Time Homeowners" at www.irs.gov. It can make it easier to benefit from all the tax advantages that come with owning your own home, such as deductible mortgage interest and real estate taxes.

Remember that a home doesn't have to be a single-family house. It can be a co-op, a mobile home, or even a houseboat if that's where you live.

ZONING RULES

Many local governments have strict building and zoning rules that may limit the additions and renovations you can make to your home. You might need to get approval or a permit from the appropriate local committee or agency before starting construction. Typically, you'll have to pay a fee, based on the estimated cost.

Home Equity Borrowing

If you need to borrow, a home equity loan usually offers the best rates, plus the advantage of tax savings.

Home equity loans let you borrow using the equity you've built up in your home as **collateral**. You can often borrow more money at a lower interest rate than with other types of loans. And, in many cases, you can deduct the interest you pay on the loan when you file your tax return, reducing the actual cost of borrowing still further. Most of the other interest you pay, on car loans or personal loans, for example, isn't deductible.

You can choose between:

- **Home equity loans, sometimes known as second mortgages**
- **Home equity lines of credit**

HOME EQUITY LOANS

With a home equity loan, you borrow a lump sum, usually at a variable rate of interest, although some fixed-rate loans are available. You pay off the debt in installments, just as you repay your mortgage, with some of each payment going toward the interest you owe and the rest toward the **principal**, or loan amount. At the end of its term, or payment period, the loan is retired.

You may have to pay closing costs on your loan, just as you did for your first, or primary, mortgage. But lenders may offer loans with no up-front expenses as part of a promotional deal. You might also be offered a **teaser rate**, or a period of low interest, as an incentive to borrow. If that's the case, the lender has to tell you the actual cost, or **annual percentage rate (APR)**, and when the temporary rate ends.

HOME EQUITY LINES OF CREDIT

Home equity lines of credit are actually revolving credit arrangements, which you can use in much the same way you use a credit card. Your **credit line**, or limit, is fixed, and you can write a check for any amount up to that limit. Whatever you borrow reduces what's available until you repay. Then you can use it again.

The terms of repayment vary, and are spelled out in your agreement. In some cases you begin to repay principal and interest as soon as you borrow, or **activate the line**. In others, you pay interest only, with a **balloon**, or one-time full payment of principal due at some set date. Or, you may make interest-only payments for a specific period, and then begin to pay principal as well.

Most credit lines have an access period, often five to ten years, during which you can borrow, and a longer payback period. The longer you take to repay, the more expensive it is to borrow.

ATTRACTIONS

- **They are easy to get**
- **The rates are usually lower than on unsecured loans**
- **The interest is tax deductible, though there may be a cap and other restrictions. Check with your tax adviser**

WHAT YOU CAN BORROW

As a general rule, you can borrow up to 80% of your equity in your home with a home equity loan. For example, if you owed $75,000 on a home appraised at $250,000, your equity would be $175,000. In most cases, you'd be able to borrow up to $140,000, or 80% of $175,000.

Some home equity lines of credit, especially those offered without closing costs or other up-front expenses, are capped at a fixed amount, often $50,000.

While you use the loan, your equity is reduced by the amount you owe. When it's paid off, your equity is restored. However, if your home loses some of its value during the loan period, you still owe the full amount you borrowed.

BEWARE THE RISK

While home equity borrowing has many advantages, it has one serious drawback: If you **default**, or fall behind on repayment, you could lose your home through **foreclosure**. That means the lender takes over the property and sells it at auction. That's true even if you've made all the payments on your first, or primary, mortgage.

That risk is the chief reason to be very cautious about using home equity borrowing—lines of credit in particular—to pay ordinary expenses. If you're using the money to make improvements in your home, pay tuition bills, or meet other major expenses, and include loan repayment as a regular item in your budget, home equity borrowing can be a wise choice. But if you're in the position of not being able to repay, you're exposing yourself to losing everything you've invested in your home—and having no place to live.

DANGERS

- **They can be very expensive when you consider total cost**
- **You risk losing your home if you default on the payments**
- **Even if the value of your house decreases, the amount of your loan stays the same**

FINDING A LOAN

Home equity loans are generally available. Banks offer them, and so do credit unions, mortgage bankers, brokerage houses, and insurance companies.

You can start by checking rates and terms advertised in the newspaper and making some phone calls to see what's available. But before you commit yourself, you should get a description—in writing—of the rates, the term, and the other conditions of the loan.

SETTING THE RATE

Each lender sets the terms and conditions of loans it makes, though the basic elements are usually similar. If the loan has a variable rate, it must be tied, or pegged, to a specific public index. The lender adds a **margin**, often several percentage points, to the index to determine the new rate each time it's adjusted. It may happen once a year or sometimes more often.

REVERSE MORTGAGES

For older people with lots of equity but limited income, a **reverse mortgage** may seem to be an appealing alternative to selling their home. A reverse mortgage allows owners to borrow against the value of their home, so that they can continue to live there. The loan does not have to be repaid until the home is no longer the borrower's primary residence. However, the borrower must pay insurance premiums and real estate taxes to keep the loan in good standing.

You can apply for insured reverse mortgages through lenders who are approved to offer Home Equity Conversion Mortgages (HECMs) backed by the Federal Housing Administration (FHA) or from a limited number of other private lenders. The amount you can borrow depends on your home's appraised value, the current interest rate, the age of the youngest borrower, and the amount of the initial mortgage insurance premium. In addition, FHA lenders impose caps on the amount they will lend.

While interest rates quoted on reverse mortgages can be similar to those for other mortgages, there are additional fees and charges that can make them more expensive than other types of loans. Lenders must provide a "Total Annual Loan Cost" disclosure that estimates the average annual cost as a percentage of the loan, and borrowers must be counseled by a HECM approved counselor. You can find a list at www.hud.gov or by calling 800-569-4287.

Regulations enacted in 2013 to protect both borrowers and the FHA require a financial assessment before a loan is approved and an escrow account in some cases. They also limit the amount that can be withdrawn in the first year of the loan.

BORROWER BEWARE

Tapping your home's equity to pay down debt or purchase things you couldn't otherwise afford is usually a recipe for disaster, as many homeowners with large outstanding loans discovered during the financial crisis that began in 2008. If you need evidence that you should learn from other people's mistakes, this is it.

BER 6, 1996

COMPARING HOME EQUITY LINES OF CREDIT

Bank	% Above Prime	Promotional Rate	Access Period	Repayment Period
First State	1.75	(None)	5 years	20 years
Regional	1.50	Prime, 1st 2 years	5 years	20 years
TriState	1.40	Prime 1st year	10 years	[illegible]

Insuring Your Home

Insurance protects your investment in your home and your mortgage lender.

When you have a mortgage loan, you must have homeowners insurance. But you'd want the insurance anyway, to protect against potential damage to your home and its contents. In the language of an insurance policy, you're buying protection against **perils**. Some policies cover named perils—the ones they specifically identify, such as fire—while other policies cover all perils except the ones they specifically exclude.

You can buy homeowners insurance through a licensed agent who sells products from several insurance companies, an agent who represents a single insurer, or directly from a company that sells its products online. What coverage costs, or the annual **premium**, can vary significantly, depending on the insurer and the type of coverage. So can consumer service, particularly when you submit a **claim** for a loss. It's important to compare several quotes from different insurers, taking both price and service into account, before you buy a policy.

HOW MUCH INSURANCE?

Insurance companies require you to cover your home for at least 80% of its value, an amount that will be less than its market value because you are not insuring the land on which the home is built. It's almost always wiser to insure for 100% of its value, an amount the insurer determines.

INSURANCE
80%
OR MORE

There's generally a formula that determines how much coverage a homeowners policy will provide for your personal possessions (sometimes called contents coverage), any other buildings on the property, and loss of use. You choose the level of coverage you want for liability in case you are sued for injury or damages that occur on the property. You may also be able buy added coverage, called **policy endorsements**, for perils, such as floods, earthquakes, or for expensive possessions, that aren't otherwise covered.

Benjamin Franklin organized the first fire insurance company in North America in 1752. It's still doing business in Philadelphia.

TYPES OF COVERAGE

If you own a single family home, there are five types, or forms, of coverage. The most basic form, which provides the least coverage, is known as dwelling fire. The most popular form, according to the National Association of Insurance Commissioners (NAIC), is the Special, which offers the most comprehensive protection. The other three are Basic, Modified, and Broad.

WHAT'S A PICTURE WORTH?
Often, the answer is a lot. It's smart to take photographs and videos of your home and its contents and store them in a secure place—either in another location or in a fire-proof, water-resistant home safe. In case of a loss, the photos can help support your claims about the value of your losses.

A Modified policy is designed for older homes with features that would make the cost of rebuilding greater than the market value of the home.

Some policies insure the **replacement value** of your home, or what it would cost to restore it, while others cover the **actual cash value**. The latter is generally less generous—and less expensive—because it may not provide enough money to actually replace your former home, having discounted its value to reflect age and use.

One of the advantages of talking to a number of agents is that you can compare their advice on the form of insurance that would best suit your needs. You may use a fee-only insurance consultant who provides advice but does not sell policies and so has nothing to gain from the decision you make.

If you're already working with a financial adviser, he or she may provide useful guidance. And, to get started, you can download a copy of NAIC's *A Consumer's Guide to Home Insurance* at www.naic.org.

THE COST OF COVERAGE

What you pay for homeowners insurance depends on a number of factors, particularly the characteristics of your home, the type of coverage, and the insurer you choose, but also on:

- Your credit history
- Your history of filing claims and the history of claims previously filed for the home
- Security systems and devices in the home
- The other policies you own with the insurer
- The deductible you choose

A deductible is the amount you're responsible for paying out-of-pocket for each loss. After you meet the deductible, the insurer pays the amount of the remaining claim it determines is appropriate. The higher the deductible you choose, the lower your premium will be. What you need to weigh is the benefit of a lower premium against the prospect of having to cover a larger portion of a loss yourself.

FAIR WARNING
You should always check an insurer's financial reputation with a rating company and any complaints about it with your state's insurance department.

AFTER A LOSS

If your insured property is damaged by one of the perils against which you're protected, you file a claim with your insurer asking for money for the repairs. The faster you file, and the more back-up information you provide, the more quickly your claim should be resolved.

If you have loss that costs only a bit more than your deductible, you may decide not to involve the insurer at all. There may be little to gain and something to lose by filing a claim. Insurers have the right not to renew a homeowners policy when its term ends, and one reason for doing so is the number of claims you have filed, even if those claims are for legitimate losses.

Once you do file a claim, the insurance company's claims adjuster will contact you to assess the damage and report the findings to the insurer. If you don't agree with the adjuster, or with the settlement you're offered, don't hesitate to object. In the worst-case situation, you can appeal the decision to your state insurance department.

Financial Planning

When you plan, you identify financial goals and develop strategies to meet them.

When you do financial planning, you're looking toward the future, specifically at building the kind of financial security you'd like to have and being able to afford the life you want to live. But to plan successfully, you also have to evaluate the present, including the financial choices you're making now. Otherwise it's too easy to find yourself making random decisions that won't move you toward your goals effectively, or that may even interfere with achieving them.

It's never too soon, or too late, to begin. Financial planning is important, whether you've just started working or are thinking seriously about retirement. And it should be a continuing process, so that you can evaluate your progress, revise your goals, and update your strategies.

Without planning, you run greater financial risks. You may not have enough money in reserve to meet expenses you're expecting, like the down payment on a home or the price of a college education. You may have to revise your retirement plans. Or you might leave your family without enough to live comfortably if something happens to you.

PLANNING STRATEGIES

In financial planning terms, creating a strategy means defining the steps you'll take to have the money you need to pay for the things you want.

To begin, you need a clear sense of what your goals are, and what they will cost. You have to evaluate the assets you already have and find ways to increase the amount you're saving and investing. While planning doesn't guarantee success, failing to plan is likely to bring disappointment.

A DEFENSIVE BACKUP

Planning is also important because it helps you anticipate and handle the obstacles that come between you and your goals.

If your investments provide a return higher than the inflation rate, you'll be in a much better position to afford the things that are important to you.

You can take advantage of tax-deferred investments to postpone taxes and make tax-exempt investments to avoid them. Trusts may also reduce the taxes your heirs will owe down the road.

With an emergency fund plus adequate health and life insurance as hedges against unexpected expenses and illnesses, you're less vulnerable to potential hardship.

DEFINING YOUR GOALS

Planning is important because it helps you identify a range of goals that you're working to achieve:

Short-term goals
You may focus on things you hope to have in a couple of years, like a new car or a new home.

Mid-term goals
You may have expenses to meet several years in the future, like tuition payments or a vacation home.

Long-term goals
You probably have hopes for a comfortable retirement, the opportunity to go places and do things you've always wanted, or a chance to provide security for your heirs.

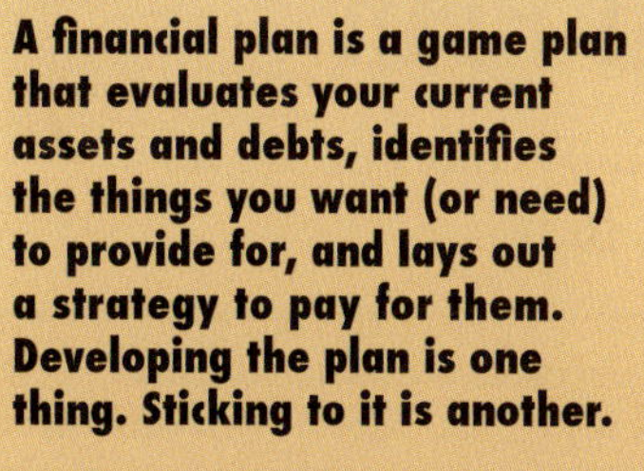

A financial plan is a game plan that evaluates your current assets and debts, identifies the things you want (or need) to provide for, and lays out a strategy to pay for them. Developing the plan is one thing. Sticking to it is another.

SIX OUT OF TEN AMERICANS rate a steady source of retirement income as their primary financial goal.

Inflation has averaged 3% since 1926.

Seek a strong return on your investments

Tax planning can help to reduce what you owe.

Choose tax-deferred and/or tax-exempt investments

Liquid investments are those you can quickly turn into cash.

Create an emergency fund with investments you can liquidate easily

SEEKING ADVICE

The biggest danger isn't making a mistake by choosing the wrong approach. It's in doing nothing. Many people take advantage of professional advice in drawing up a financial plan and putting it into action. You can work with an adviser from the beginning, consult a number of different advisers, or choose someone to execute the decisions you make on your own.

In fact, a major advantage of working regularly with an adviser is the added incentive it can provide to get started and stay focused. Help is increasingly available, too, as all types of financial institutions compete to provide the services their customers are looking for.

Among the places you can turn to for help with financial decisions are:

- **Registered investment advisers (RIAs)**
- **Certified public accountants (CPAs)**
- **Financial planners**
- **Insurance brokers**
- **Brokerage firms**
- **Lawyers**

Making a Financial Plan

A financial plan is a working document that can be as flexible or as focused as you want it to be.

Whether you work with an adviser to create a plan, use computer-based software, tap into a financial planning site on the Internet, or devise one on your own, you'll need to use some basic financial documents to establish your starting point. Advisers, for example, usually ask to see recent income tax returns, a summary of your investments, information on your retirement plan, and your life insurance policies.

Some advisers develop a detailed written plan, also called a personal financial analysis. The document summarizes the information you've provided, includes an overview of various financial planning strategies, and recommends specific investments or other steps you should take to achieve your objectives.

If you prefer, you can request a simpler approach, and receive a letter summarizing the goals you're working toward, the approach to investing you want to take, and the type of investments the adviser recommends.

1 Your Current Financial Situation
2 Financial Goals
3 Making a Financial Plan
4 Paying for College
5 Planning for Retirement
6 Social Security
7 Wills and Trusts
8 Estate Planning

OWNERSHIP: ONE OF THE KEYS TO PLANNING

The kind of ownership you select for property and other assets determines what you can do with them, how vulnerable they are to creditors, and what happens to them after you die. Laws are complicated and vary from state to state, so you should seek professional advice.

Type	Features
Individual (or sole)	• You own the asset outright
Joint tenants with rights of survivorship	• You share the asset equally with one or more joint owners • At your death, the assets automatically transfer to joint owner(s) • You generally can't sell property without consent of joint owner(s)
Tenants in common	• Each owner holds a part, or share, of the whole • Individual shares can be sold, given away, or left as owner wishes
Tenants by entirety	• You must be married • Mutual consent is needed to divide or sell the property • At death the property goes to the surviving owner
Community property	• In the nine states with community property laws, most property acquired during marriage is owned equally by both partners • Once property becomes community property, it remains so even if you move out of the state

Choosing an Adviser

If you're looking for a financial adviser, you'll want to set up some criteria to help you evaluate the people you may work with. Among the questions you can ask to help you make a choice:

How much experience have you had working with clients that share my situation and goals?
Ten years of experience isn't too much to expect, especially if you're new to investing.

What's your background and expertise?
You'll want to work with an adviser who has a strong reputation in the field, either as an individual or as an employee of a respected company, and appropriate credentials.

What kinds of investments do you sell most often?
Be wary of an adviser who emphasizes one or two types of investment products instead of a broader range of traditional and perhaps some alternative investments.

How are you paid?
Some advisers are paid commissions on the products they sell, some receive flat or hourly fees for their service, and some are paid a combination of fees and commissions.

Will you explain how the investments you recommend will help me achieve my goals?
You'll want an adviser who's willing and able to explain how investments work and why they're suited to your needs.

How will I know if my investments are producing the results I want?
Advisers should provide regular reports on the status of your accounts and be willing to explain how well your investments are performing and what adjustments to consider.

THE RISK ISSUE

Financial planning almost always involves making investments. One issue you'll have to resolve is the kind of investment risk you're comfortable taking. The choice ranges from very little to a great deal, with a broad middle ground between the extremes.

Conservative investors tend to protect their principal to the extent that's possible while still realizing enough return to outpace inflation. They may prefer insured certificates of deposit (CDs), US Treasury issues that they hold to maturity, and securities such as high-rated bonds, blue-chip stocks, and balanced mutual funds.

Aggressive investors are willing to put their principal at greater risk for the potential of realizing a higher return and greater growth. They may invest in new or troubled companies, higher-risk bonds, and a range of alternative investments.

Moderate investors emphasize growth over safety, though they typically prefer to limit the percentage of their portfolio assets committed to higher-risk investments. They may select a variety of securities and other products, including some alternative investments.

The risk of investing too conservatively is limiting your ability to realize your goals. But investing too aggressively, especially as you get older, increases the potential for losing money in a market downturn without leaving time to recoup your losses. That's risk you may not want to take.

BEATING INFLATION

Conquering the effects of **inflation**, or the gradual increase in what things cost, is one reason financial planning is so important. Because prices rise, money doesn't buy as much this year as it did last. Ten years from now, it will buy even fewer of the things you need.

That means to maintain the same standard of living, you need an equivalent increase in income every year. One way you may achieve that is by investing money so it earns more than the rate of inflation, even after you've paid the taxes on your earnings. What you have left of your earnings after inflation is called your **real rate of return**.

ASSESSING PROGRESS

At least once a year, you and your adviser should evaluate the investments you've made to see if they're providing the return you expected. If not, it may be time to make some changes to your portfolio. But keep in mind that what's happening in securities markets will have a major effect on how individual investments perform.

If the economy is healthy and the markets are prospering, your investments should reflect that strength. But if investments overall are lagging, yours are likely to lag as well. A diversified portfolio of investments helps you manage some of the market risk that every investor faces, though it doesn't guarantee a positive return.

Managing Your Cash Flow

With planning, you can manage your spending to cover immediate needs and still invest for long-term goals.

Your finances are in constant motion. Even as money comes in from employment and other sources, it goes out for regular living expenses like food and shelter, and for periodic bills like taxes and insurance.

This in-and-out movement is called your **cash flow** and the spending plan you create to manage that flow is called a **budget**. Budgeting has a bad reputation because it's often equated with denying yourself things you want. But it's an essential part of financial planning and not as difficult or restricting as you might think.

HOUSEHOLD BUDGETS

Using last year's expenses as a base, you estimate how much you will spend this year for housing, food, transportation, and so forth—including the large bills like insurance that you pay quarterly or annually.

If your expenses are higher than your income or you want to invest more, you can review what you're spending to see where you can cut back. The simpler and more realistic your budget, the more likely you are to follow it.

REGULAR EXPENSES

Weekly	Food, transportation, household supplies, childcare
Monthly	Housing, utilities, phone, loan repayments
Quarterly/ annually	Insurance, taxes
Other	Medical and dental expenses, repairs, entertainment

THE PART INCOME PLAYS

Your income determines the amount you can afford to spend on the necessities and pleasures of life. To keep your cash flow positive, which means having money left at the end of a pay period to spend as you wish, you may want to allocate income first to those essentials that have a fixed price, such as housing and loan repayments. You can then allocate to essentials with variable costs, such as food and clothing, where you can reduce your spending more easily if you are running short.

FINDING MONEY TO INVEST

If you'd like to invest more of your household budget, but aren't sure how to get started, consider these suggestions:

IT DOESN'T TAKE MUCH
To create an emergency fund, multiply your monthly take-home pay times six to find the amount you want to save. Then decide how much you can reasonably afford to put aside each pay period to reach that amount as quickly as possible.

FUNDS IN RESERVE

Irregular income, unexpected repair bills, medical expenses, or loss of your job can pose special cash flow problems. It pays to have a safety net—customarily six months of living expenses—set aside in an **emergency fund**.

You can use your credit card to cover some emergencies when they happen, but interest charges will increase the cost dramatically if you repay over an extended period. If you can withdraw from your emergency fund when the credit card bill is due, you can combine the convenience of charging with the economy of paying in full.

Whatever the reason you need money from your emergency fund, you should replenish it as quickly as you possibly can, even if it means sacrificing some immediate pleasures. It's the only way to be prepared for the next emergency.

TRACKING YOUR SPENDING

To budget effectively, you have to know where your money is going. It's relatively easy when you pay bills electronically or by check, since you have a record. Your credit card statement can be helpful as well, with each charge and amount listed. What's harder to track is the cash you take at the ATM—and it's often cash spending that gets you into budget trouble because it can be hard to track.

You might keep a daily spending record for several weeks, using either an app on your smartphone or a small notebook. You may be surprised at what you discover about where your money goes.

If you have children, encourage them to be part of the budgeting process, from allocating income to various family expenses to keeping track of spending. It's a great way to learn about money.

1. Have a percentage of your salary deducted from your paycheck and invested in an employer sponsored retirement plan.
2. Write a regular investment check when you pay your bills each month.
3. Invest any money you get from gifts, bonuses, or extra jobs.
4. Reinvest all the money you make on your existing investments, automatically if you can.
5. Pay off your credit card balances. Then put an amount equal to what you were paying in interest into an investment account.

Your Net Worth

Your net worth statement is a snapshot of where you stand financially at a given point in time.

Assets WHAT YOU OWN

Cash reserve assets include the money in your checking, savings, and money market accounts, CDs, Treasury bills, and the cash value of your life insurance policy.

Investment assets include stocks, bonds, mutual funds, retirement plans, annuities, and other investment products.

Personal assets are your possessions. Some — like antiques, stamp collections, and art — may **appreciate**, or increase in value. Others — like cars, boats, and electronic equipment — **depreciate**, or decrease in value over time.

Real estate includes your home and other land and buildings.

Assets

CURRENT ESTIMATED VALUE	for example
Cash in banks & money market accounts	$20,000
Amounts owed to you	0
Stocks/bonds	$14,000
Mutual funds	$15,000
Certificate of deposit (CDs)	$8,000
IRAs	$40,000
Employer retirement accounts (vested interest)	$135,000
Real estate:	
Home	$200,000
Other	0
Business interests	0
Personal property*	$30,000
TOTAL ASSETS	**$462,000**

* Includes furnishings, jewelry, collections, cars, security deposit or rent, etc.

THE STARTING POINT

As part of deciding how to pursue your financial goals, you should take a look at where you stand right now. You do that by adding your **assets**—such as cash, investments and retirement plans—in one column and your **liabilities**—or debts—in the other. Then subtract your liabilities from your assets to find your **net worth**.

Net worth doesn't measure cash flow, but there's a clear relationship between how you spend your money and what your financial picture looks like. If your assets outweigh your liabilities, you have a positive net worth. If your liabilities are larger, you have a negative net worth.

If your net worth is negative, turning it around by paying off short-term debt should be your financial planning priority.

If it's positive, you'll want to look at how your assets are divided among cash, investments, and real estate and perhaps make some changes. Your age, goals, and amount of risk you're comfortable taking are important factors in determining the most appropriate focus. For example, if you're starting your career, it may be growth in your investment portfolio, or, if you're nearing retirement, a combination of growth and income.

FAIR MARKET VALUE
When you're calculating what your personal assets are worth, the number to use is their fair market value. That's the price a willing, rational, and knowledgeable buyer would pay for things you are willing to sell.

Liabilities

WHAT YOU OWE CURRENTLY AND LONG TERM

Liabilities

AMOUNT	**for example**
Mortgages	$160,000
Bank loans	0
Car loans	$7,000
Lines of credit	$3,000
Charge accounts	$1,800
Margin loans	0
Alimony	0
Taxes owed:	
Income	$21,000
Real estate	$3,200
Other	0
Other liabilities	
College loan	$7,000
Insurance	$3,500
Business loan	0
TOTAL LIABILITIES	**$206,500**

Short-term debts are your current bills: credit card charges, installment and personal loans, income and real estate taxes, and insurance. Your present credit card balances are generally included, even if you regularly pay your entire bill each month.

DEED **Long-term debts** are mortgages and other loans that you repay in installments over several years.

OTHER PERSPECTIVES
When potential lenders assess your application—which includes a net worth statement—to decide whether you qualify for a loan, they look at what you already owe. But they may also calculate what you might owe if you charged as much as you could on all your credit cards and drew on all your potential lines of credit.

What most lenders like to see is a net worth statement that shows substantial savings and investments, and limited debt. Investments mean that you have resources to tap in an emergency, including assets that could be sold to pay your debts.

NET WORTH

ASSETS MINUS LIABILITIES

USING NET WORTH STATEMENTS
Figuring your net worth is not only a critical first step in financial planning. It will also come in handy in many financial situations. For example:

- Mortgage lenders require a statement of your assets and liabilities as part of the application
- College financial aid is based on your net worth, so you'll have to report your assets and liabilities when your children apply
- Loan and line-of-credit applications usually require net worth statements
- Certain high-risk investments may require that you have a minimum net worth — often $1 million or more

Paying for College

Once you fit all the pieces together, you'll have a clearer view of how funding your child's education works.

There's no doubt that the cost of higher education has increased dramatically in recent years. Yet, perhaps surprisingly, the number of students enrolling in all types of institutions has increased as well. One reason may be the recognition that a college education makes financial sense. Another may be the commitment—and sometimes sacrifice—that families are willing to make in order to pay for the opportunity that education provides. But a third, and possibly equally powerful factor, is that families can turn to a number of sources to help them cover the cost of college.

But it's equally true that while saving may not be easy, there are a number of programs designed not only to encourage you to put money away for college but to provide tax benefits if you do. In fact, you may already have a plan to accumulate the money you anticipate needing.

Among the most widely available choices are those that share the **529** label: college savings plans, state prepaid tuition plans, and the private college prepaid plan. Another alternative is the **Coverdell education savings account (ESA)**, which has lower contribution limits but more flexibility in choosing investments. You may also

THE ROLE OF SAVING

Whether you're a brand new parent or you've had lots of practice as a mom or dad, this probably isn't the first time you've thought about saving for college. It's hard to avoid the bottom line: Colleges and universities, as well as the federal government, consider it your responsibility to contribute to your children's higher education expenses. Without at least some savings, meeting that obligation may not be possible.

COLLEGE RESOURCES

You can look to a number of websites for help in planning for your child's education.

- **www.collegeboard.com** Information on college costs, scholarships, and entrance exams.
- **www.studentaid.ed.gov** Guidance on the process of applying to and paying for college.
- **www.collegesavings.org** Valuable information about 529 savings and prepaid plans.

realize tax savings in certain cases by paying college expenses with interest you earn on US savings bonds.

Better yet, you don't have to select just one method. You can create a savings plan that combines several of the options and takes advantage of their most attractive features.

IT'S A GRANT WORLD

It's the unusual person who doesn't enjoy receiving a gift. And the best gift a college student—and his or her parents—can receive is a grant or scholarship. Grants directly reduce the amount of your child's education expenses and, unlike loans, never have to be repaid. Grants make up about 40% of all financial aid that college students receive. About half of the grants in any year come from private institutions and individual colleges and universities, while others are provided by public institutions, including certain states and, in the case of **Pell grants**, the federal government.

One challenge may be determining the requirements a student must meet to qualify for a grant. Certain grants, such as Pells, are need based. Others are merit based, which means they're given in recognition of the student's achievement. Still others may take both the student's merit and need into account.

In most cases, students are offered grants after they've been accepted at a college or university, but sometimes a school or organization will offer a grant as an incentive to attract your child. You can check with the high school guidance office and organizations you belong to for a list of potential scholarships. You might also discover lists online—though few of these lists are really useful. Beware of sites that ask you to pay a fee to access their files: There's no reason to pay to find scholarships.

COST OF BORROWING

!

BUYING TIME

Unlike grants, higher education loans must be repaid. Like other loans, they accumulate interest, so that borrowers end up repaying more than the amount they actually spend on tuition, room, board, and other expenses. But the federal government offers both parents and students guaranteed loans that can reduce—though not eliminate—the costs of borrowing.

You and your child must complete a comprehensive federal loan application, the FAFSA, to qualify for an undergraduate loan. But the good news is that federal loans have made it possible for many more students to afford a college education.

Federal loans—**Stafford** for students and **PLUS** for parents—are available directly from the government. You can find detailed information on what loans are available and how to apply at www.studentaid.ed.gov, a US Department of Education website.

You can borrow money elsewhere as well, which you may opt to do if federal funding doesn't meet your needs. One of the issues you'll have to weigh in accumulating loans—even for a good cause—is the long-term responsibility they impose on you and on your child.

MAKING COMPROMISES

The other thing to remember about paying for college is that there are many routes to an undergraduate degree.

While some students finish their college education at one school within four years, many don't follow that pattern. For instance, students may begin at a local two-year public college and then transfer to another public institution or to a private college. They may attend school part-time throughout the year for five or six years rather than full-time during the fall and spring semesters for four years. Or they may select a school that expects students to combine time in class with paid internships.

Certain circumstances may also provide you with different ways to reduce the overall cost of your child's education. For instance, someone in your extended family might provide housing for your child to live off campus at a school he or she wants to attend, perhaps in return for doing certain chores. Or your child may accumulate advanced placement credits or take some required courses in the summer to reduce the length of time it takes to graduate.

Obviously, decisions such as these must be collaborative or the likelihood of their being successful is slim. But if you and your child can talk frankly about your shared goals and the financial realities, you can find a way to achieve what you both want.

529 Savings Plans

Once you know how 529 plans work, you'll be ready to pick the plan that's right for you.

Opening a 529 account couldn't be easier: You can enroll in a plan by simply completing a brief application and making a minimum contribution. Many plans allow you to enroll online through their websites, or you can complete an application with your financial professional.

But that doesn't mean you should enroll in a 529 plan blindly. Every plan is a little different, so you should research the key features of each plan you're considering. Then you'll be sure to find the plan that works best for you.

THE ROSTER

Several key players make each 529 savings plan work:

- Individual states **sponsor** 529 savings plans. They're also responsible for choosing a plan manager and determining the rules and limits surrounding their plan.
- The **plan manager**, which may be a mutual fund company, brokerage firm, or insurance company, handles all transactions and investments within your account.
- As **account owner**, you're responsible for naming a beneficiary, making contributions, choosing an investment track, and managing withdrawals.
- Your **beneficiary** can attend any accredited US college, vocational, or graduate school to which he or she is admitted.

CONTRIBUTING

Contribution limits vary from plan to plan and often reach $300,000 or more. And, if you approach the contribution limit of one plan, you can always open another in the same beneficiary's name.

You can make contributions in lump sums or in regular installments. They can work equally well, so you can choose the approach that suits your financial situation.

Making contributions in installments may put less strain on your overall budget. But the amount you end up with depends on how much you put in each month—and how your investments perform.

On the other hand, making lump-sum contributions creates a larger investment base, which means the potential for faster growth over a long period of time. But large contributions are usually not fully eligible for a state tax deduction, and annual gifts of more than $14,000 per beneficiary in 2014—or $70,000 once in five years—could require you to file a gift tax return for the year you make the contribution.

Any earnings in your account are determined by how the assets are invested, what the return is, and what you pay in fees.

PROFESSIONAL HELP

You can open a 529 college savings plan directly or with the advice and assistance of an investment professional. Someone with experience in evaluating plans can help you analyze the investment tracks, compare pros and cons, and perhaps provide the encouragement you need to enroll. Some professionals work on a fee-only basis, while others earn a commission if you buy a specific plan through them.

If you buy directly, you assume responsibility for doing your own research and choosing the plan that's best for you. One advantage is that the overall cost is likely to be less.

THE SUN DOESN'T SET
A 529 savings plan beneficiary can use the assets in the plan at any qualifying institution, including graduate or professional school. There's no age limit. Or, at any point, you can switch the beneficiary to any member of the extended family.

STAY ON TRACK

When you contribute to a 529 savings plan, your plan manager pools your money with that of other plan participants to invest in a portfolio that's allocated according to a specific investment track. You can choose from among different investment tracks provided by your plan manager:

- **Age-based tracks** gradually reallocate to shift the investment focus from growth to preservation as your beneficiary nears college age. You can usually choose an aggressive, moderate, or conservative age-based track, which determines how your portfolio is invested initially.
- **Fixed tracks** remain the same over time. While these tracks are often either 100% equity or 100% fixed-income, you can choose several different fixed tracks to allocate your assets.

Depending on the plan you choose, you may be able to switch investment tracks as often as once every 12 months or put new contributions in a different track. With certain plans, you may also be able to customize your account by choosing from among different investment options within each track. And if your plan's investments consistently perform below your expectations, you can switch plans once every 12 months.

MAKING WITHDRAWALS

Withdrawals from a 529 savings plan are tax free as long as they're used to pay for your beneficiary's qualified education expenses, which include tuition, books, fees, school equipment, room and board, as well as any technology needs.

You can arrange to have your beneficiary's qualified expenses paid directly by your plan, or you can pay the expense yourself and request reimbursement later. Either way, it's up to you to match all qualified expenses with withdrawals when you file your federal income tax return each year. Your plan will provide an annual statement that details your contributions, earnings, and withdrawals for the year. If your withdrawals exceed your qualified expenses for the calendar year, you'll have to calculate the percentage of earnings on which tax and penalty payments are due.

CHOOSING THE RIGHT PLAN

Here are some questions that may help identify the plan that's best for you:

- Does the plan offer investment choices that suit your needs?
- How much will you owe in enrollment, sales, and annual fees?
- Can you deduct contributions from your state income tax?
- Will earnings be exempt from state income taxes if you invest in this plan?
- Does the plan accept out-of-state participants?
- How have the plan's investments performed in the past?
- How long are you required to hold an account?
- What are the minimum and maximum contribution limits?
- Can anyone contribute to the plan?

You may want to start by looking at the plans offered by your own state, since tax benefits may be especially appealing if your state income taxes are high to begin with.

Planning for Retirement

It's never too early to take retirement seriously.

You can start saving for retirement as soon as you begin earning income. It's a smart move even if your retirement is many years in the future. You can take advantage of savings plans that allow you to defer taxes on your earnings, and sometimes on your contributions, or to avoid taxes entirely if you follow the rules.

There are two categories of tax-saving retirement plans: those offered by employers and **individual retirement accounts (IRAs)** that you open on your own. Even if you're part of an employer plan, you can contribute to an IRA, taking advantage of both ways to accumulate retirement assets.

In addition, you may want to invest in taxable accounts to make your retirement even more financially secure. You have more flexibility at every stage, from adding money to taking it out. And while you'll owe taxes on your investment income, the rate you pay on much—though not all—of it will be lower than the rate you pay on ordinary income.

EMPLOYER PLANS

Employers may sponsor a retirement plan for their employees if they wish. There are two basic plan types, and most employers offer one type or the other, though some employers offer both.

A **defined benefit plan**, better known as a pension plan, promises a certain level of income when you retire. The way your pension is calculated is described in the plan and is usually based on what you're earning at the end of your career, the number of years you work for the employer, or frequently both. Your employer contributes to and manages the pension fund to produce the return it needs to make the pension payments owed to you and other plan members.

In a **defined contribution plan**, you, your employer, or both contribute money to a retirement account in your name. The retirement income you'll receive is not guaranteed. Rather, it depends on the amount that's contributed, the way the contributions are invested, and the return the investments provide over time.

One advantage of a defined contribution plan is that it's often **portable**, which means you can take your account balance with you if you change jobs. That's not the case with defined benefit plans.

BEING PART OF THE PLAN

If your employer offers a pension plan, you're generally included in the plan automatically, though you may have to be on the job a minimum length of time, be a full-time employee, or both, to be eligible.

Participation in a defined contribution plan is generally voluntary, so you may have to sign up. Increasingly, however, employers are automatically enrolling everyone who is eligible and offering the alternative of dropping out. In most, but not all, defined contribution plans, you defer a percentage of your pay, which is deducted from your paycheck. These contributions are invested in the investments you select from among those available through the plan—typically mutual funds, managed accounts, target date funds, company stock, and fixed income investments, although other choices may be available.

If you're enrolled automatically, the percentage you contribute is set initially by the plan, as is the way your contribu-

THE PLANS AT A GLANCE

There are several varieties of defined contribution plans, including the ones mentioned here. With all except SIMPLEs, contribution limits are the same and balances can be moved between plan types if you change jobs. The type of plan you're eligible for depends on where you work.

401(k)
- All employees of businesses that sponsor plans
- Matching contributions optional

403(b)
- Employees of nonprofit, tax-exempt organizations
- Matching contributions optional

Section 457
- State and municipal workers
- No matching contributions

Thrift Savings (TSP)
- Federal employees and employees of companies offering plans
- Matching contributions for federal employees, others optional

SIMPLE
- Employees of companies with fewer than 100 workers
- Matching contribution required

tions are invested. But you always have the right to contribute more if you wish, up to the annual limit that applies, and to choose any of the other investments available through the plan.

ON YOUR OWN WITH AN IRA

IRAs are voluntary, so you must take the initiative to open your account with a bank, brokerage firm, mutual fund company, or insurance company, and contribute as much as you wish up to the annual limit. The financial institution where you open your IRA is its **custodian**, which involves holding the account assets, acting on your instructions to buy or sell investments, and providing regular statements of your IRA's value. But a custodian has no responsibility for the choices you make.

As with defined contribution plans, what your IRA is worth when you're ready to retire depends on the amount you have contributed, the investments you've chosen, and the way those investments have performed. Timing is also a factor, since the longer contributions compound, the greater they have the potential to grow.

KNOW YOUR LIMITS

Congress sets an annual maximum on contributions to employer plans and IRAs, though what you contribute to an employer plan doesn't reduce the amount you can to put in an IRA, or vice versa. You don't have to contribute the full amount that's permitted, but, the more you can afford to put away, the larger your account has the potential to grow over time.

If you're 50 or older, you're entitled to make additional **catch-up contributions** even if you've contributed the maximum every year you were eligible. The added money can give your account value a boost.

Contribution limits, or caps, which are higher for employer plans than for IRAs, are indexed to inflation and may increase as frequently as every year. In some years, they're unchanged, but they have never been reduced. For example, in 2014, the cap for most defined contribution plans is $17,500 plus $5,500 catch-up, while IRA caps are $5,500 and $1,000 catch-up. Different limits apply to defined benefit plans and certain small-company defined contribution plans.

Employer Plans

Retirement savings aren't just nice to have. They're essential.

When you choose to participate in an employer's retirement savings plan, that's just the first of several choices you'll make. You'll also need to decide how much you'll contribute as well as select investments from the plan's menu. And that's not all.

A number of employers who offer a tax-deferred 401(k), 403(b), or TSP also offer a tax-free Roth alternative. The Roth has the same annual contribution limit, menu of investment alternatives, and **required minimum distributions (RMDs)** after you turn 70½ that tax-deferred accounts have. But there are also significant differences.

With a Roth, you contribute after-tax income—rather than pretax income as you contribute with a tax-deferred account—so your current tax bill is not reduced. However, you can withdraw any earnings in the account free of federal income tax provided you are at least 59½ when you leave your job or retire and your account has been open at least five years. The contributions aren't taxed at withdrawal either since you've already paid the tax. With a tax-deferred account, on the other hand, you pay income taxes on all withdrawals at the same rate you pay on your ordinary income.

You may be able to divide your contribution between a Roth and a tax-deferred account, and you can convert a tax-deferred balance to a Roth, although you'll need to pay the tax that's due. But you can never transfer money from a Roth to a tax-deferred account. If you choose a Roth, any employer matching contributions go into a parallel tax-deferred account.

TERMS AND CONDITIONS

As a condition of participating in a retirement plan and postponing taxes or, with a Roth, avoiding them entirely, you agree that you won't withdraw from your plan account before you reach at least 59½, though you may qualify for an exception if you retire between 55 and 59½.

You may be able to borrow from your account balance if your plan permits loans. The loan, plus interest that is charged at market rates, is repaid with regular deductions from your salary. However, if you leave your job, you must repay any outstanding loan balance in full almost immediately or it is considered a withdrawal and becomes taxable.

A ROTH FOR YOU?

Whether or not a tax-free Roth is a wise choice for you depends on your age, your current tax rate, what you anticipate will happen to tax rates in the future, and the other types of retirement investments you have. It may pay to consult you tax and investment advisers before making this decision.

DISTRIBUTION BASICS

When you take a new job or retire, you can leave the balance of your retirement account with your previous employer, roll it over to a new employer's plan if the plan accepts rollovers, or roll it into an IRA. All three alternatives maintain the tax-deferred status of the assets.

The option that's best for you depends on a number of factors, including the investment choices available, the administrative and management costs, and personal preferences. It can be smart to consult an independent financial adviser as well as the human resources office where you work to seek comprehensive, unbiased advice.

If you're leaving your job for any reason, including being let go or retiring, you also have the right to take a lump sum distribution in cash, though it's rarely a good idea. Any taxes that have been deferred must be paid when you file your tax return for that year. In fact, 20% of the amount you ask to withdraw will be withheld to cover what you'll potentially owe to the IRS. What's more, you could be liable for a 10% tax penalty on the entire withdrawal if you're younger than 59½.

If your account is in an employer's plan or you've rolled it over to a tax-deferred IRA, you generally must begin to take **RMDs** when you reach 70½. The amount you must withdraw each year is determined by your age and the balance in the account at the end of the previous plan year, which is often, but not always, December 31.

The exception is that you can postpone withdrawals if both of these conditions apply:

- **You are still working for the employer sponsoring the plan**
- **You or your spouse don't own more than 5% of the company you're working for**

WHEN THE VEST FITS

If you've been part of an employer's retirement plan and leave your job for any reason, what happens to your account? That depends on the type of plan it is and how long you've participated.

You're entitled to benefit from your participation if you're **vested**, meaning you've worked for the employer for the required **vesting period**. The vesting period for each type of plan is set by federal law, and can never be longer than six years for a defined contribution plan or seven years for a defined benefit plan. It can be shorter at the employer's discretion.

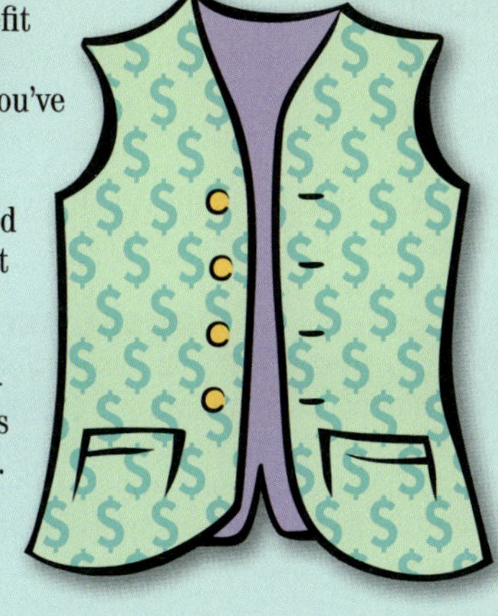

In a defined contribution plan, vesting requirements do not apply to any money you contributed or the earnings on those contributions. That amount is always yours. But if you're vested, you have the right to any matching contributions your employer made plus any earnings on those contributions.

If you're vested in a defined benefit plan, you'll be eligible for a pension when you're old enough to qualify, based on the employer's rules. It's worth keeping track of any pension accounts, as the income could be a welcome addition to your retirement budget, even if it's only a modest amount.

IRAs: What They Are

IRAs are easy to set up—but not always easy to understand.

IRAs, or individual retirement accounts, are tax-deferred, personal retirement plans. You can contribute every year you have earned income whether or not you participate in an employer's retirement plan. There are two types: the traditional IRAs, to which contributions may be deductible or nondeductible, and the Roth IRA.

- All **traditional IRAs** are **tax deferred**, which means you owe no tax on your earnings until you withdraw
- **Roth IRAs** are also tax deferred, so you owe no tax on your earnings as they accumulate. Withdrawals will be **tax free** if you follow the rules

WEIGHING THE CHOICE

If you have a choice of which IRA to open, you'll want to weigh the pros and cons:

	ROTH	TRADITIONAL IRA	
		Nondeductible	Deductible
PROS	• Tax-free income at withdrawal • No required withdrawals	• Tax-deferred earnings • No tax due on contributions at withdrawal	• Immediate tax savings on tax-deductible contributions • Tax-deferred earnings
CONS	• AGI limits • Not deductible • Requirements to qualify for tax-free withdrawal	• Not deductible • Tax due at regular rates at withdrawal • Required withdrawals beginning at 70½	• Tax due at regular rates at withdrawal • Required withdrawals beginning at 70½

DO YOU QUALIFY FOR A ROTH IRA?

		You qualify for a Roth	Partial Roth	You don't qualify for a Roth
SINGLE	Adjusted Gross Income	$114,000		$129,000
MARRIED	Adjusted Gross Income	$181,000		$191,000

A SWEET DEAL

The only requirement for opening an IRA is having earned income—money you make for work you do. Your total annual contribution is limited to the annual cap. That's $5,500 in 2014, whether you choose a traditional IRA or a Roth. If you're 50 or over, you can also make an additional annual catch-up contribution of $1,000.

Any amount you earn qualifies, and you can contribute as much as you want, up to the cap. But you can't contribute more than you earn.

SPOUSAL ACCOUNTS

If your husband or wife doesn't work, but you do, you can put up to the annual limit into a separate spousal IRA in addition to your own contribution. The advantage for the nonworking spouse is being able to build an individual retirement fund.

WHICH IRA FOR YOU?

In addition to having earned income, you must qualify to deduct your contributions to a traditional IRA or contribute to a Roth IRA. The rules are different in each case.

If you're single, you qualify for a fully deductible IRA contribution when you file your federal income tax return if you were not covered by an employer sponsored retirement plan during that year. If you were covered by a plan, you may be able to deduct some or all of your contribution based on your modified adjusted gross income (MAGI).

If you're married and file jointly, either of you can deduct your own contribution if you are not covered by a retirement plan at work. But if either of you is covered by a plan, the other's right to a deduction is reduced gradually if your joint MAGI is over $181,000 and eliminated if it's over $191,000 in 2014. If you're both covered, the limits are $96,000 and $116,000 in 2014.

Deductions are gradually phased out if you are covered by a retirement plan

Single taxpayer

$5,500
$0
$60K Income
$65K
$70K

Married filing jointly

$5,500
$0
$96K Income
$106K
$116K

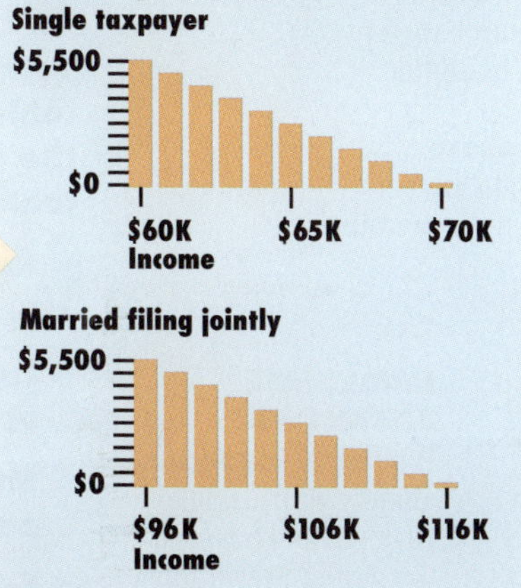

For 2014.

Eligibility for a Roth IRA is based on your filing status and MAGI, with higher income limits for married couples filing a joint return than for single filers. If you qualify to make a partial contribution to a Roth, you can put the balance in a traditional IRA. Married couples filing separate returns usually aren't eligible either to deduct contributions or contribute to a Roth.

While you can't deduct your contribution to a Roth IRA, taxes on earnings in your account are deferred as they accumulate, and you make tax-free withdrawals if you qualify. In most cases, that means you are at least 59½ and have had your account open at least five years before you withdraw.

IT'S YOUR ACCOUNT

It's easy to open an IRA. All you do is fill out a relatively simple application provided by the mutual fund company, bank, brokerage firm, insurance company, or other financial institution you choose to be **custodian** of your account.

Because IRAs are self-directed, meaning that you decide how to invest the money, you're responsible for following the rules that govern the accounts. Basically, that means putting in only the amount you're entitled to each year. You must also report your contribution to a traditional IRA to the IRS, on Form 1040 or 1040A if it's deductible and on Form 8606 if it's not.

You can invest your IRA money any way that is available through your custodian including individual securities, funds, and bank products. The things you can't buy are fine art, gems, non-US coins, and collectibles. And you can sell investments in your IRA account without paying tax on your gains until you withdraw from your account, but there may be transaction costs.

IRA

January
1 First day to deposit lump sum

April
15 Last day to deposit for prior year

WHEN TO CONTRIBUTE

You have until the day taxes are due—usually April 15—to open an IRA and make the contribution for the previous tax year.

You can contribute to your IRA in a lump sum or spread the deposit out over the year. You may put in the whole amount the first day you can, January 1 of the tax year you're making the contribution for, to give your money the longest time to grow. If you're like most people, you're more apt to make the deposit on the last possible day. The most practical solution may be making contributions on a regular schedule.

Annuities

Tax-deferred annuities are another way to build your long-term retirement savings.

When you purchase an **annuity**, or long-term insurance company contract, no taxes are due on your earnings until you begin to receive income under the terms of your contract. There are no contribution limits on annuity investing as there are with IRAs or employer-sponsored retirement plans. That means you can build a substantial nest egg for your long-term needs. However, putting money into an annuity doesn't reduce your salary or income tax the way tax-deferred employer plans do.

Building Up

You can choose a **single premium annuity** with a lump-sum purchase, or build your annuity account by adding money regularly over a period of time. During this **accumulation phase**, while the money is invested and you are not withdrawing, you pay no taxes on earnings in the account.

DEFERRED ANNUITIES

With a deferred annuity, you get the benefit of tax-deferred compounding for an extended period, at either a fixed or variable rate. When you're ready to begin withdrawals, the way you'll collect is spelled out in the terms of your contract. Usually it's in regular monthly installments, but it may be in a fixed number of lump-sum payments. The part of your payout that comes from earnings is taxed at your regular tax rate.

OR

IMMEDIATE ANNUITIES

You buy an immediate annuity with a single payment and begin the payout period right away, or within the first year. The amount of each payment is set by the terms of your contract. In the sense that an annuity provides regular income, usually after you retire, these plans resemble employer sponsored pensions. You can also buy an immediate annuity to provide a lifetime stream of income for another person.

Annuity Agreement

Your annuity contract defines the terms and conditions:

- **Amount of premium**
- **Earnings at fixed or variable rate**
- **Method of payout**
- **Fees and other investment costs**

LOOKING AT THE BOTTOM LINE

Annuities are popular ways to save for retirement, but they also have critics who argue that other investments give you more for your money. It pays to look at both sides:

Pluses

- Tax-deferred compounding
- Guaranteed income stream with fixed-rate contract based on claims paying ability of issuer
- With variable annuities, there is opportunity for growth of principal that may keep up with or exceed the rate of inflation

Minuses

- Some variable annuity contracts have high fees and other expenses
- Some annuities impose stiff surrender charges
- Taxes are due at regular income-tax rates, not the capital gains rate
- Income from fixed-rate contract may not keep up with inflation

FIXED OR VARIABLE?

Deferred annuities are available in two forms: those that pay a **fixed rate** of interest for the life of the annuity and those that pay a **variable rate**.

When you buy a fixed annuity contract, the insurance company that issues it guarantees payment of a fixed rate of return during the build-up period and a guaranteed income for life if you **annuitize**, which means converting your annuity into a stream of income. The company invests your principal and takes responsibility for paying as promised. But actual payment depends on the issuer's ability to meet its obligations.

With a variable annuity, you decide how your money will be allocated among a specific menu of **subaccounts**, or annuity funds, offered by the issuer. Subaccounts are pooled investments, similar to mutual funds, with varying objectives and strategies. Variable annuities give you the chance to potentially earn more than you could with a fixed rate. However, the contract makes no payment promises, so you could also end up earning less if the markets are weak or you choose poorly performing funds.

Paying Out

You start collecting on your annuity investment during the **payout period**, usually after you retire. If you're 59½ or older when payments begin, you owe income tax on your earnings. If you're younger than that, you'll usually have to pay an additional 10% of the withdrawal as a penalty.

MONTHLY PAYMENTS

You can get regular monthly payments for as long as you live or for a set period of time, such as ten or 20 years.

OR

LUMP-SUM PAYMENT

Or you can end your contract and take a cash distribution. You may lose money if your plan imposes a penalty for early withdrawal.

IMMEDIATE ANNUITY PAYOUTS

The most common payout options for both deferred and immediate annuities are:

Single life, which pays a set sum per month as long as you live. When you die, the payments stop.

Life or period certain, which covers your lifetime or a set number of years, whichever is longer. Your heirs get the balance if you die before the term is up.

Joint and several, which makes payments for your lifetime and the lifetime of your joint annuitant.

WEIGHING THE ISSUES

Immediate annuities provide the security of a regular income for people who are uncomfortable managing their investments. But they have some potential drawbacks:

- If you choose a single life annuity and die within a few years, the company keeps the balance of your money and your heirs get nothing
- Your annuity income may not keep pace with inflation
- The seller, usually an insurance company, may not fulfill its part of the contract

CHECKLIST FOR ANNUITY INVESTORS

✓ Consider annuities only if you're investing for the long term. Withdrawals before age 59½ face a 10% penalty tax, plus income tax.

✓ Investigate the reputation of the company offering the annuity to be sure it's sound.

✓ Compare surrender periods. Most annuities have surrender charges in the first seven years. You can avoid annuities with lifetime surrender charges.

✓ Look beyond the initial rate if buying a fixed-rate annuity. Approach unusually high rates with caution.

✓ Look for maximum flexibility on getting your money out. You can avoid annuities that don't offer a lump sum or give you a lower interest rate if you take one.

✓ Research the fees and annuity charges and avoid paying more than 1.5% to 2% annually.

✓ Compare costs. Some annuities cost more than others offering a similar rate and income stream.

Social Security

For more than 70 years, Social Security has been a source of monthly retirement income.

Social Security was introduced in 1935 in the aftermath of the Great Depression to provide a safety net of regular income to retired and disabled workers and their families. It's a mandatory plan, requiring most employees, their employers, and the self-employed to contribute a percentage of their salary to support the program. In return, they, their spouses, and sometimes their dependents are eligible for retirement, disability, and survivorship benefits.

The program has been updated and expanded over the years, to include more workers and provide added benefits. Medicare, the healthcare plan for people over 65, was added in 1966. In 1972, benefits were indexed to inflation, so that as the cost of living goes up, your Social Security payments increase too.

BUILDING A RECORD

When you enroll in Social Security, your account is open though it isn't activated until you begin working. Then, every year the amount you contribute is recorded. Because what you'll ultimately collect is based on what you pay in, it's important that the record is accurate.

The Social Security Administration creates a Social Security earnings statement if you are 25 or older and haven't yet begun to collect payments.

You can access a copy of your current statement by creating a secure, password-protected account at www.ssa.gov/myaccount. The statement reports what you've contributed each year and estimates the monthly benefit amounts you'll qualify for at retirement or if you're disabled. If you're already collecting benefits, you'll find both your earnings and to-date payment histories.

If you discover your record is wrong—and it sometimes is, especially if you work more than one job—you can ask that it be corrected. You'll have to supply some evidence for your claim, such as the W-2 income-reporting forms that you file with your income tax. With that information, you should have no trouble correcting the problem. In fact, the SSA encourages people to check their annual earnings records carefully, since recent errors are easier to fix than long-existing ones.

> To be eligible for Social Security benefits, you must contribute to the system for a total of ten years or be the spouse or dependent of someone who does.

FINDING HELP

You can call the SSA helpline at 800-772-1213 for assistance. Or, you can make an appointment at your local Social Security office. Either way, you should have copies of your most recent statement and back-up evidence to support your claim. It's not a speedy process, but it's worth the time.

PUTTING MONEY IN

Every year you earn income, you and your employer are taxed equal percentages of your earnings, as required by the Federal Insurance Contribution Act (FICA): 6.2% up to an annual earnings cap for Social Security and 1.45% of your total earned income for Medicare. If you're self-employed, you pay both parts but can

Social Security estimates that slightly more than 25% of 20-year-olds will become disabled before they turn 67, double the percentage who will die within the same time span. For most, the only disability insurance for which they'll be eligible will come from Social Security.

We've Got Your Number

When you're registered with Social Security, your nine-digit number usually stays the same for life, even if you change your name.

The first three digits indicate the state where you applied for a card. The number changes as more cards are issued in that state.

The second group of digits doesn't have a particular meaning — though they are related to the order in which cards are issued in a region.

The last four digits are assigned in numerical order, for example 7091, 7092, 7093, and so on. One exception: Twins, triplets, or other multiple siblings don't get numbers in order.

987-65-4320

deduct half the total when you file your federal tax return for the year.

To be eligible for benefits, you need to accumulate a total of 40 credits over your working life. You acquire credits at the rate of up to four each year for earning at least the required per-credit minimum dollar amount, which is reset each year. For example, in 2014, you gain one credit for each $1,200 you earn. But whether you earn $4,800 or $480,000 during the year, you can't accumulate more than four credits.

GETTING MONEY OUT

People born before 1938 could collect full Social Security benefits when they turned 65. But **full retirement age (FRA)** has increased to 66 for anyone born between 1943 and 1954 and will increase again gradually for anyone born between 1955 and 1959 until it reaches 67 for those born in 1960 or later.

You can collect a percentage of your benefit if you retire at 62. But if you work beyond your full retirement age and keep on contributing, the amount of your benefit increases 8% each year until you reach 70.

When you die, your surviving spouse is entitled to your benefits unless he or she would collect more on his or her own work record. The exact amount your spouse will be eligible for depends on what you were collecting and how old he or she is.

CALCULATING BENEFITS

Unlike most pensions, which calculate your benefit based on what you're earning at the end of your career, Social Security counts what you earn over most of your working life, specifically the 35 years in which you earned the most. As with other pensions, though, the more you've earned, the higher the amount you'll receive.

Although the dollar amount of your benefit is based on your average earnings, the percentage of earnings your benefit will replace is higher for people who earned less over their lifetimes, in keeping with the mission of providing at least a basic level of financial support.

You can use the Retirement Estimator at www.ssa.gov to calculate a sense of the benefit you can expect to receive based on your earnings record and the age at which you apply for benefits. However, this is just an estimate. Your actual benefit could vary, based on how long you continue to pay into the system, what your future earnings are, and any changes to the system itself.

TAXING BENEFITS

If your total income for the year, including half your Social Security and your tax-exempt earnings, is greater than the level set by Congress, you owe federal income tax on part of your Social Security benefits. The higher your total income, the greater percentage of your benefit is taxable, to a maximum of 85%.

About 20% of people getting Social Security benefits end up paying tax on part of what they receive. The Internal Revenue Service (IRS) provides a worksheet you can use to figure out exactly how much of your benefit you must include in your taxable income. If you pay estimated taxes, you'll have to be sure your installments cover what you'll owe.

Life Insurance

Evaluating your life insurance needs is a key part of financial planning.

The simple answer to how much life insurance you need is enough money to cover your dependents' immediate cash needs and living expenses.

If you support a family, keep a household running, have a mortgage, or expect your kids to go to college, insurance can fill the financial gap left by your death or disability. But if you don't have dependents, or they don't need your money to live on, your insurance needs may be very different.

Older people may need less insurance if their financial obligations have been met—mortgages and college tuition are paid—and their investments are producing income. But insurance may provide an important benefit for a surviving spouse or to cover potential estate taxes.

One rule of thumb says that you need five to seven times (or even ten times) your annual salary. But a lot depends on your personal situation, dependents, and other sources of income.

A FEW THINGS A FEE-ONLY INSURANCE ADVISER CAN DO

- Provide second opinion about policies you're planning to buy
- Tell you whether your existing insurer is financially sound
- Evaluate whether your existing policy or annuity is appropriate
- Help you select policies and choose options and riders
- Negotiate lower commissions from your insurance agent

CALCULATING NEED

Life insurance calculators, which you can find on a number of financial company websites, can be a good first step in helping you estimate the amount of coverage you need. But they can't take you, as an individual, or your unique needs, into account.

You'll need to determine the expenses you want the policy to cover. These may include the immediate costs related to your death, your dependents' current

ROUGHING OUT YOUR LIFE INSURANCE NEEDS

To estimate the amount of coverage you need to replace 75% of your take-home pay for the years you would have been working, multiply your salary by the factor at the intersection of your salary and your current age. In this example, it's $720,000.*

Annual pay	Current age of person insured						
(before taxes)	25	30	35	40	45	50	55
$30,000	14	13	12	10	9	7	5
$40,000	13	12	11	10	9	7	5
$60,000	12	12	11	9	8	6	5
$80,000	12	11	10	9	8	6	4
$100,000	11	10	9	8	7	5	4
$150,000	10	10	9	8	7	5	4
$200,000	9	9	8	7	6	5	5

*Doesn't take into account any income survivors can expect from Social Security, investments, or other sources. More or less coverage may be needed, depending on individual family circumstances.

Source: Principal Financial Group

living expenses, and specific goals, such as settling large outstanding debts, supporting elderly parents, or paying for college educations. Your investment assets may offset some of these needs, and your survivors may have income and assets of their own. So you'll want to consider this information in figuring the coverage you need.

Equally important, you'll need to choose a policy whose premiums fit within your budget. If you buy a policy you can't afford or that restricts your ability to cover other expenses, you're more likely to let the policy lapse, putting your dependents' security at risk.

Keep in mind, too, that the type of coverage and the death benefit that are right for you at one stage in your life may not be appropriate at another. For example, while you have a mortgage and your children are young, you may need much more insurance than you do later. Changing needs are a good reason to make an insurance review a part of a regular reassessment of your financial plan.

UNDERWRITING is the process insurance companies use to assess you as a risk and decide if they will sell you insurance. It's based on the information you provide in the application. If you don't tell the truth, your insurance may be cancelled, or the company may refuse to pay a claim.

PAYING THE BILL

The cost of buying life insurance varies enormously, depending on the type you buy, the company you buy it from, and how long the company thinks you are likely to live.

Estimating the total cost can be tricky, since the **premium**, or amount you pay for some types of insurance, may increase over time. Further, two companies may charge very different amounts for the same coverage.

One way to do a search is to use a fee-only adviser, who can help you sift among the options and select the one that's best for you. As a rule, life insurance provided through your employer is the least expensive, but may provide only a portion of the amount you need.

RISK vs. COST

The cost of life insurance is largely determined by the risk you pose to the insurance company, as shown on an actuarial table. These tables project your life expectancy based on age, gender, health, and life style.

If you're considered a high risk—for example, if you smoke, are overweight, or have a dangerous occupation or hobby—the company may charge you a higher premium than other people of the same age or gender, or refuse to insure you at all.

However, if you are a nonsmoker whose health and life style make you likely to live longer, you may qualify for lower rates that significantly reduce your premium and save you money.

Types of Life Insurance

You can buy life insurance that protects you for a limited period of time or stays in effect until you die.

All life insurance is alike in several ways. You pay **premiums** to a life insurance company in exchange for its promise to pay a certain amount of money, called the **death benefit**, to the **beneficiary** whom you designate when you buy the insurance. The death benefit is also known as the face value. The contract between you and the insurer is known as a **policy**, and it spells out the terms of the coverage.

If you own the policy, you are the **policyholder**. The rights of ownership allow you to:

- Change the beneficiary or add other beneficiaries
- Assign, or transfer, ownership to someone else
- Borrow from the policy's account value, if it has one

If you're the person whose life is covered by the policy, you're the **insured**. You can be both the policyholder and the insured, or you can own a policy on another person's life, provided you have what's known as an **insurable interest**. In brief, that means you would suffer financial hardship if that person died. Similarly, someone with an insurable interest could own a policy on your life.

In most cases, the beneficiary owes no income tax on the death benefit that's paid when the insured dies.

TYPES OF INSURANCE

Your policy may last for a specific **term**, or period of time, and may be renewable. Or you can buy a **cash value** policy, also known as permanent insurance, which means it covers you for as long as you're alive, or at least until you turn 100. With either term or cash value insurance, you must pay your premiums on time to keep the policy **in force**. If you fail to pay, the policy **lapses** and no death benefit will be paid if you die.

TERM INSURANCE

As long as you pay the premium, you're covered.

If you die, your beneficiaries receive the death benefit.

If you stop paying the premium, the policy ends and you get nothing back.

TERM INSURANCE

Term insurance is the simpler and, at least initially, less expensive coverage. In exchange for your premiums, your policy covers you for a specific period, which could be as long as 20 or 30 years. If the policy is renewable, you may extend for an additional term without having to demonstrate you're in good health. However, many policies are not renewable after you reach a specific age, such as 75. At each renewal, the premium increases.

If you die during the term, and your policy is in force, the insurer pays the face value. But if you are alive when the term ends, and you don't renew, you are no longer insured.

Term policies may be convertible. In that case, you can turn your term policy into a permanent policy with the same death benefit, generally without having to demonstrate that you are in good health. The premiums for a convertible plan are usually higher than for regular term.

INSURANCE ONLINE

An insurance company's website can be a valuable resource, especially if you want to learn more about the various types of life insurance the company offers. There may be a calculator to help you estimate the coverage you need. And if you purchase a policy, you'll probably be able to manage your account, make payments, or report a claim online.

CASH VALUE INSURANCE

As long as you pay the premium, you're covered.

If you die, your beneficiaries receive the death benefit.

If you stop paying the premium, you get the cash surrender value.

COMPARING ALTERNATIVES

If you're not certain whether term or permanent insurance is right for you, it may help to think about how you would answer these questions:

- Is a cash value account an effective way to save for your goals or might investments be better choices?
- What's the comparative cost of purchasing the amount of coverage you need?
- Do you anticipate that your insurance needs will change significantly in the foreseeable future?
- Is there any reason to think you may be less insurable in the future than you are now?

CASH VALUE INSURANCE

Cash value insurance combines a death benefit with a **cash value account** funded with part of each premium you pay. Earnings on the account's assets are tax deferred. If you die while the policy is in force, your beneficiary receives the death benefit, which includes the balance in the cash value account.

If you end your policy before you die, the insurer will subtract any outstanding loans you've taken against your cash value account, plus outstanding interest and any fees, and send you the remainder, called the **cash surrender value**. No death benefit will be paid.

If the policy has been in force for a number of years, it's possible that the amount you receive will be larger than the premiums you paid. If that's the case, you'll owe income tax on the difference between your cost and what you received, calculated at the same rate you pay on ordinary income.

TYPES OF POLICIES

Despite the seemingly endless varieties, there are two basic types of cash value insurance:

1. **Whole life**, sometimes called **straight life**, is the most traditional. The premiums stay the same for the length of the policy. Once you've paid all the premiums, the policy remains in effect until you die or, in some cases, turn 100. You accumulate a cash reserve, but you have no say over how the money is invested.

2. **Universal life** offers some flexibility. You can vary the amount of the premium by applying a portion of the accumulated savings to cover the cost. You can also increase or decrease the amount of the death benefit while the policy is in force. But you pay for this flexibility with higher fees and administrative costs.

Typically, there's a guaranteed rate of return on the savings portion for the first year, and a minimum, or floor, for the life of the policy.

Long-Term Care

Many people are concerned about long-term healthcare for themselves or their parents.

When you're doing financial planning, you have to think about some of the things you'd rather not consider, such as needing long-term healthcare. You may also be concerned about the costs of taking care of aging parents or disabled children.

Among the things that make planning for healthcare more complicated than accumulating tuition money or buying a home are its unpredictability and its expense. You don't know if you'll need care at all, or when, or for how long. And since healthcare costs have tended to escalate more quickly than most other expenses, it's difficult if not impossible to predict what you'll spend.

There are four ways to address long-term care in your financial plan, since ignoring the possibility you'll need care can have dire consequences:

1. You can self-insure, which means you will pay for care yourself, an approach that works best if your net worth is $5 million or more.
2. You can count on family members or friends to provide care that Medicare doesn't cover.
3. You can anticipate relying on Medicaid after you have exhausted your resources.
4. You can buy long-term care insurance to help cover the cost.

QUALIFYING FOR BENEFITS

Some long-term care policies pay benefits if your doctor considers it necessary. Other policies pay only if the insurer's medical examiner agrees.

In most cases, the issue is whether you are able to manage what are described as the **activities of daily living (ADLs)** independently. These include getting in and out of bed, moving around, eating, bathing, and using the toilet. What you want is a policy that considers you eligible when you have problems with just two ADLs rather than three or more.

You should think twice before buying a policy that requires hospitalization prior to qualifying for benefits, since many people who need the coverage have chronic, deteriorating conditions that don't necessitate a hospital stay. In addition, consider the policy's restrictions on the qualifications that care providers must have. If you want more flexibility in selecting providers, you may be willing to pay for a policy that provides it.

Other issues to consider are the length of time you will be eligible for benefits, often two to five years, and the elimination period, or how long you'll have to wait after qualifying for payments to begin.

LONG-TERM CARE INSURANCE

Long-term care insurance provides coverage for chronic illnesses and long-term disabilities that aren't covered by Medicare. Look for policies that pay for nursing-home care, care at home, and hospice or respite care for the terminally ill and their families.

In most cases, people think about buying the coverage in their 50s, or 60s, when the premiums are still affordable. By then, they may be able to trim life insurance premiums, freeing up the money to pay for it.

If you're considering the coverage, you'll want to examine what various policies pay as well as what they cost. Make sure that your plan provides coverage for cognitive diseases such as Alzheimer's. Also check your plan's restrictive policies on payouts, prior conditions, and other factors.

You'll also want to ask about inflation protection. While having it will probably add to the cost, the advantage of an inflation-indexed plan is that what you get at the point you begin to use the insurance will be more in line with your real costs. A plan that may cover a large part of the daily nursing home cost this year will probably cover much less of the total bill ten years from now.

The most affordable coverage is generally available through group policies provided by your employer or some other association you belong to. You can get individual coverage from life insurance companies, too, though it may be expensive.

THINGS TO CHECK FOR

If you're buying long-term care insurance, you'll want to ask these questions:

- ☑ What's the waiting period before payment begins?
- ☑ Does the plan cover cognitive diseases?
- ☑ Is there **inflation protection**?
- ☑ Is there a **waiver of premium**, which allows you to stop paying while you're using the benefits?
- ☑ Is there a **nonforfeiture clause**, so that you'll get partial coverage or your heirs will get money back even if you let the policy lapse?
- ☑ How often are policies revoked after they are issued?

LONG TERM CARE

LINKED BENEFIT POLICIES

One alternative to traditional long-term care insurance is a life insurance policy that accelerates, or prepays, the death benefit if you need long-term care. This approach may be especially attractive if you're financially secure and like the idea that, if you use only a portion of the death benefit to cover your care, your heirs will receive the balance. That doesn't happen with a long-term care policy.

Estate Planning

Your estate contains the assets you have accumulated by the time of your death.

While much of the financial planning you do is designed to help you and your loved ones live the life you want, one aspect of it, called **estate planning**, deals with what happens to your assets after you die. There are many ways to ensure that they're transferred to the people or institutions you want to benefit, and that potential hassles are minimized or avoided.

The actual value of your estate isn't calculated until after your death, but, using your current net worth statement, you can arrive at a fairly accurate estimate as you start the planning process.

Some assets, including those you own jointly, your retirement accounts, and the face value of your life insurance will go directly to your joint owner(s) or the beneficiaries you have selected. Other assets must be given away while you're living or transferred by will, trust, or other legal document.

The advice of an experienced lawyer who specializes in trusts and estates is always valuable and often essential to achieve your goals.

THE TAX ISSUE

While the most important aspect of estate planning is allocating your assets to your heirs, you can't ignore the potential for estate taxes. Under current law, federal taxes are due on net estates valued at more than $5 million plus an annual inflation adjustment. In 2014, for example, the amount is $5.34 million. A net estate is what's left after subtracting tax-exempt bequests—including those to your spouse and qualifying charitable institutions—as well as the cost of settling the estate from the estate's gross value.

Those assets that pass directly to beneficiaries—life insurance, retirement plans, and half the value of property you own jointly with your spouse—are included in your estate when it's valued. So are assets in any revocable trusts you have created, your share of a partnership or other business, and money you're owed.

While only a very small percentage of estates owe the federal tax, individual states may impose estate or inheritance taxes, or both, that are assessed against much more modest estates.

DEFENSIVE MEASURES

There are some strategies you can use to reduce the value of your estate and so the potential for estate taxes.

Tax-free gifts. You can give gifts of up to $14,000 to as many people as you wish each year, totally tax free. If you're married, you and your spouse can give twice that, or $28,000. Gifts to your spouse are always tax free, provided he or she is a US citizen. There's an annual cap if that's not the case. Gifts to qualifying charitable institutions are also tax free, though the annual amount you can give may be limited to a percentage of your adjusted gross income.

Paying education or medical bills. You can pay another person's tuition or medical bills not covered by insurance without incurring gift tax or reporting the payment to the IRS if you pay it directly to the educational or medical institution to which the money is owed.

Insurance. If someone other than you owns the life insurance policy on your life, the death benefit won't be included in your estate. If you are the current policyholder, you can assign ownership to another person, have your spouse or child buy a new policy on your

MAKING GIFTS

In addition to your annual tax-free gifts, you can give away assets worth up to $5 million plus an annual inflation adjustment during your lifetime, though any part of the exempt amount you gift reduces the amount you can transfer free of federal tax at your death.

You have to report gifts over $14,000 per person to the IRS using Form 709 when you file your tax returns for the year the gifts are made, but no tax is due until the total reaches the cap. And the government doesn't care how you share your assets—all as gifts, all as bequests, or a combination.

Gifts you make to a relative at least two generations younger than you are, such as a grandchild or great-grandchild, may be subject to special generation-skipping, and somewhat complicated, tax rules.

POWER OF ATTORNEY

You may want to consider granting a durable or springing power of attorney to someone who could handle your finances and other matters if you were too ill or disabled to make your own decisions. You should consult with your lawyer about the pros and cons as well as the process.

life, or, if you have a very large estate, use a life insurance trust.

Irrevocable trusts. If you move assets into a trust that you don't control and can't change, their value is no longer part of your estate. But you need professional help to create effective trusts, whether assets are transferred to them while you are alive or after your death.

Of course, any money you spend is no longer part of your estate either, though things you buy with the money will be if they have monetary value.

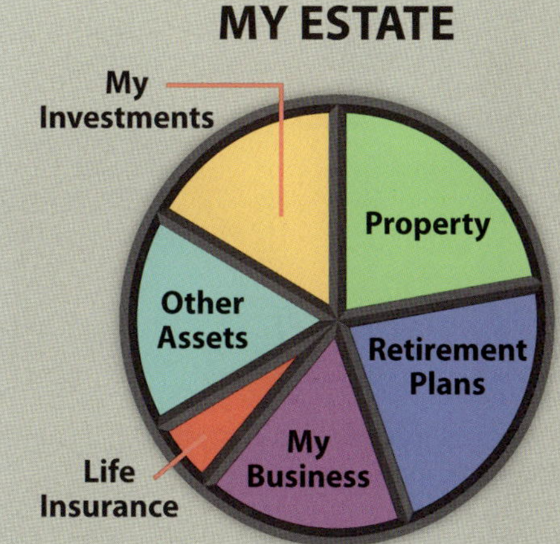

GIVE IT OR WILL IT?

If you're deciding whether to give someone a gift while you're alive or leave the property in your will, there are some things to consider, including the tax consequences.

	Outright gift	Inheritance
Value for income tax purposes	Value is what you paid for it originally.	The value is **stepped up**, or increased to what the property is worth at the time of inheritance.
What taxes are due	Potentially capital gains tax on increased value will be due when property is sold. No inheritance tax due. Potential estate tax can't reduce size of gift.	Capital gains tax if property is sold likely to be less than if received as gift. Inheritance tax may be due. Estate tax might reduce the size of the inheritance.

Making a Will

A will is the primary tool in an estate planning toolbox.

A will is a legal document that allows you to transfer your property at your death to your **beneficiaries**.

The document details your bequests, identifying the recipients as specifically as possible and describing what each one is to receive. It's generally wiser to leave major bequests as percentages of your estate's value rather than as dollar amounts, as you can't be sure what the value will be at the time of your death.

In preparing your will, you name an **executor** who will be responsible for carrying out the terms. The executor may be your spouse, an adult child or children, a different relative, a friend, or sometimes a third party, such as a lawyer. If you have minor children, you also name a **guardian**, who will assume responsibility for them if their surviving parent is not able or willing to care for them, or if you and your spouse die at the same time. Ideally, parents name the same guardian in their separate wills.

It's also a good idea to identify contingent executors and guardians in case your first choices are unable or unwilling to serve—though you should never name anyone who has not agreed to take on this responsibility.

Beneficiaries Guardian Executor

MAKING IT LEGAL

State laws spell out what's required to make your will official, but laws vary from state to state. If you change your primary residence, you should create a new will even if the provisions remain the same.

You execute the will by signing it in the presence of two, or sometimes three, witnesses, who also sign it to attest to the fact that you said it was your will and they watched you sign it. The witnesses don't have to read the will or be told what it says. However, in some states, a witness may not inherit anything that's included in the will, and in others people mentioned in the will may not serve as witnesses. Other rules may apply as well, which is why working with a lawyer based in the state where you live is essential.

You should sign just one copy of the will and file it with your lawyer, at home, or in some other secure place, making sure to tell your executor where it is. A safe deposit box is not a good choice as it may be sealed at your death.

WILL POWER

A signed and witnessed will is valid but it is not written in stone. You can make changes any time you want, provided you ensure that you're following required procedures. If it's a relatively minor change—even if it has major consequences for one or more beneficiaries—

ONE AT A TIME

Whenever you create a new will, you should destroy the signed copy of any previous will. More than one signed will can create probate problems, even if one is clearly more recent than the other. Unsigned copies or photocopies are not official and can be useful for reference.

you can use a **codicil**, a legal document that amends an earlier one. The codicil must be witnessed and should be attached to the existing will.

What a will can't do is transfer jointly held property—which goes directly to the joint owner. Nor can it transfer assets in insurance or annuity contracts, employer sponsored retirement plans, or individual retirement accounts (IRAs), which go directly to the beneficiary you have named in the contract or plan document. It's important to keep those designations up to date, just as with your will, especially when there is a major change in your life, such as a marriage, a divorce, or the birth of a child.

The other thing you can't do in a will is disinherit your spouse unless there is a valid prenuptial or postnuptial agreement that spells out what he or she receives if you die or the marriage ends. In fact, every state requires you to leave your spouse at least a minimum percentage of your estate's value. In community property states the rule may be somewhat different, as each spouse automatically owns half of all marital property.

In all states except Louisiana you can disinherit your children, but you may want to specify that you are doing so. Otherwise, a child who was omitted could claim you simply forgot.

THE PROBATE QUESTION

Any property that is transferred by will is subject to **probate**, which is the legal process of proving, or verifying, your will. Depending on the state, the court that handles verification is called probate court, orphans court, or surrogates court. While it's sometimes a routine matter, especially for small estates, probate can be slow, sometimes perverse, and often costly, which give it a bad reputation.

A clear, unambiguous will has the best chance of surviving the probate process intact in case it is contested. The most difficult situations generally involve disinherited children and parents who have been involved in a contentious divorce.

While you can smooth the probate process by using a **living trust** to transfer most of your property, you can't avoid it entirely. You still need a will to handle the property that isn't in the trust and name an executor and, if need be, a guardian.

NO WILL?

Without a will, you die intestate. The court decides what happens to your assets, without having to take your wishes into account. It's wishful thinking if you believe otherwise.

Trusts

Trusts shelter money for your heirs and provide for those who can't fend for themselves.

Trusts are legal entities—like corporations—that earn income, pay taxes, and hold assets. The trustee administers the trust, making investment decisions, paying taxes, and distributing the assets. You can give the trustee the authority to match the distributions to the specific needs of your heirs. For example, you might identify funds for paying tuition or buying property.

The trust can make regular distributions, or it can be set up as an **accumulation trust**, which retains and reinvests the income it earns for future distribution.

You can establish a trust for anyone you want to provide income for: your spouse, elderly parents, your children, or a close friend. For example, a trust might last for a parent's lifetime, until your children reach age 28, or until your grandchildren finish college.

ADVANCE PLANNING

Trusts can be effective estate-planning tools in many different circumstances. But it is important to understand the different types of trusts and how they can work for you.

The trust or trusts that are appropriate depend on what you want or need to accomplish: complicated bequests, financial management, or tax savings. No single trust can do it all.

You might use trusts to handle transfers that can be complicated if you use a will. For example, if you own property in a state where you don't live, you can streamline the probate process by putting the property into a living trust and passing it directly to your heirs.

If you want to leave money to people you're not sure can handle the responsibility, you can use a trust as well. Then the trustee can control how the assets are

HOW TRUSTS WORK

The Donor

- Sets up the trust
- Names the beneficiaries
- Names the trustees
- Transfers property to the trust

The Beneficiaries

- Receive the assets in the trust according to its terms

TYPES OF TRUSTS

There are three major types of trusts:

1. **Inter vivos** or **living trusts** are set up while you are alive. When you die, the trust's assets are distributed to your beneficiaries according to the trust's terms.

   You can serve as trustee yourself, though you usually name a joint or successor trustee to administer the trust when you die or if you are no longer able. A living trust can strengthen your intended beneficiary's claim to potentially disputed property, as it is much more difficult to contest a trust than a will. Trust provisions can also be kept private. A will is a public document.

2. **Testamentary trusts** are created by your will when you die and are funded by your estate. They are administered by trustees, whom you name in your will.

3. **Pour-over trusts** combine aspects of both types: They are established while you are alive specifically to receive assets, like life insurance benefits, that are paid at your death. They can also receive assets specified in your will.

CAN YOU CHANGE A TRUST?

A trust can be **irrevocable** — which means you can't make changes once it's set up — or **revocable**, meaning you can modify the terms over time. Their features are:

Irrevocable Trusts

- No changes to provisions permitted
- You cede control over assets
- Assets no longer part of your estate
- You cannot benefit from assets
- You can add but not remove assets

Revocable Trusts

- You can modify them until you die
- You control assets and pay the taxes
- You can transfer assets in and out easily with no annual limits
- Assets included in your estate

The Trust

- Earns income
- Pays taxes
- Holds assets

The Trustees

- Control the property in the trust
- Manage the trust's investments
- Oversee distribution of assets

paid out. Or you can have a trustee control how assets are divided among a number of different beneficiaries, depending on their circumstances or whatever criteria you establish.

CRUMMEY POWERS

By creating a trust using Crummey powers, you can take annual gift exclusions for money you contribute to create or fund a trust. It works if the beneficiary—even a minor child without a guardian—has the power to withdraw the gift within a fixed time period, often 30 to 60 days from when the gift was made. The beneficiary must be notified of that right, and the money must be on hand to be withdrawn if the option is exercised.

If the beneficiary leaves the money in the trust, it can be reinvested for potential future growth. You choose the time at which the trust will end and the assets become the beneficiary's property. Until then, you or someone you name acts as trustee and manages the trust for his or her benefit.

TRUSTS FOR SPECIAL PURPOSES

A **bypass trust**, also called an exemption-equivalent trust, is funded with assets that are valued at up to the amount you can leave to people other than your spouse free of federal estate tax at the time of your death. The actual dollar amount is not specified as it can change. The trust pays your surviving spouse the income from the trust. But the trust itself is not part of his or her estate. When your spouse dies, the assets pass to your heirs. No estate taxes are due, even if the total accumulated value has grown to more than the amount you could leave tax free. Your spouse can set up a similar trust for assets in his or her name, effectively doubling your tax-free estate.

A **qualified terminable interest property (QTIP) trust** leaves your estate to your spouse in trust, but lets you control its disposition after your spouse's death. Your spouse receives the trust income, but cannot use the principal or change the beneficiaries you have designated.

A **charitable remainder trust** benefits a specific charity—eventually. It has the double advantage of a lifetime income from the trust's investments for you (or your beneficiary) and tax deductions the year you contribute to the trust. At your (or your beneficiary's) death, the principal goes to the charity.

A **charitable lead trust** benefits a particular charity, which receives income generated by the assets in the trust for the term of the trust. When the term ends, your heirs get back what remains. You can value the gift at a reduced rate, based on IRS tables, and save on estate taxes because the benefit to your heirs is delayed.

A **life insurance trust** is set up while you are alive to own your life insurance policy. Your death benefit is paid to the trust. But you should seek expert legal advice before using this approach.

Health Insurance

Having the right healthcare coverage requires advance planning.

Illness and injury can put a major strain on your physical and emotional health. And, unless you have adequate insurance, either can undermine your financial security. The challenge is to understand the coverage options available to you so you can choose one that best fits your healthcare needs and financial situation.

Most people who work full-time for a mid-sized or large employer, and many who work for a small business or non-profit organization, have health insurance as an employee benefit. If you don't have employer-provider insurance, you must buy individual coverage for yourself and your family. If you're 65, or if you have certain disabilities, you'll probably be eligible for Medicare, the federal health insurance program. But unless your spouse is also eligible, he or she will need separate insurance.

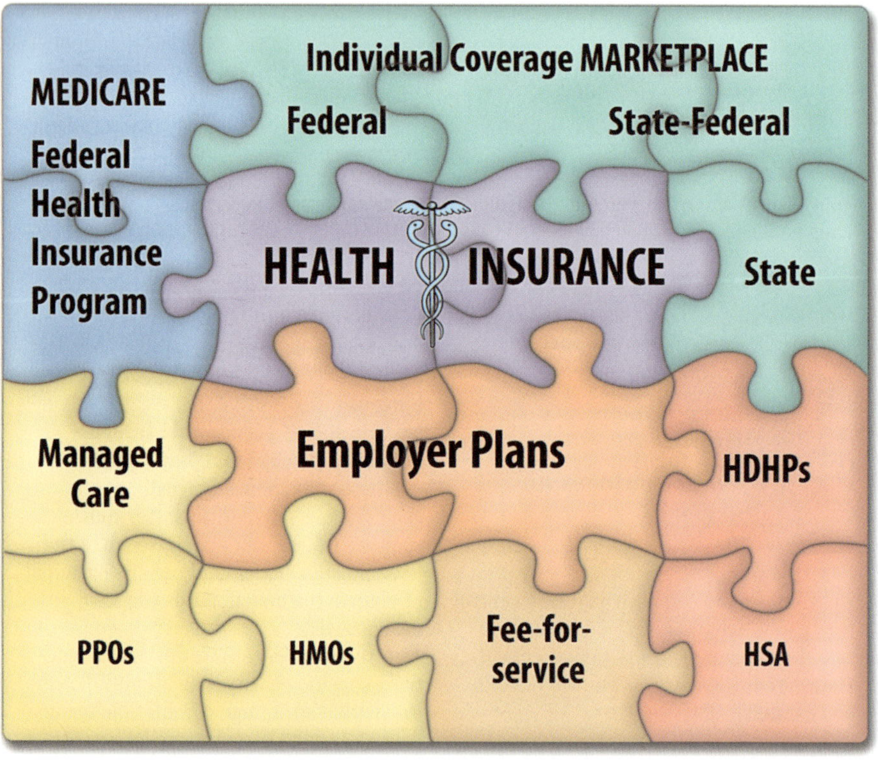

EMPLOYER HEALTH PLANS

If you have coverage through your employer, you may have a choice of plans, including **managed care** plans, **fee-for-service** plans, and a **high deductible** plan (HDHP).

In managed care plans, which could be either **preferred provider organizations (PPOs)** or **health maintenance organizations (HMOs)**, you have access to a roster of participating doctors. A PPO negotiates a fee for each service with the healthcare providers in the plan, and your cost is whatever share of the **premium** your employer requires you to pay plus a **copayment** for each visit. Most preventive care is fully covered. The copayment is a fixed dollar amount that the plan sets, often one amount for your primary care provider and a higher one for specialists. If you see a provider who doesn't participate, your plan may or may not pay a percentage of the cost.

An HMO, on the other hand, employs the plan's doctors and other providers and often owns the hospitals to which you are admitted. Typically, visits to other doctors or facilities aren't covered.

In a fee-for-service plan, you can see any doctor or service provider you wish.

MAJOR CHANGES

The Affordable Care Act (ACA) has made major changes in healthcare coverage, and more changes are scheduled to phase in through 2020. Among the most notable are these:

- Insurers must cover everyone who applies, including people with pre-existing conditions who were previously uninsurable
- All plans must provide free preventive care and at a minimum must cover at least ten essential benefits, including emergency care, maternity care, and mental health
- Dollar caps on lifetime and yearly coverage have been eliminated
- Insurers must spend 80% of the premiums they receive on medical care or provide rebates
- Children may remain on a parent's employer-provided plans until they turn 26
- Employers with 50 or more full-time workers must provide insurance that covers a minimum of 60% of healthcare costs with a premium of no more than 9.5% of the employee's income
- If you have individual coverage, it can't be cancelled if you stay current on your premiums

However, if your plan was created before March 23, 2010, its terms are **grandfathered**, and these newly mandated provisions do not apply.

THE ACA DEBATE

The ACA is controversial, to put it mildly. In that way it is reminiscent of both Social Security and Medicare, two federal social programs that were bitterly contested when they were enacted. Though these are now popular programs, what will happen with the ACA remains to be seen.

Your insurer will pay a percentage, typically between 70% and 80% of the cost it approves for the specific treatment. That may be less than the amount you were charged. You pay your share of the premium and must meet an annual **deductible**, after which the insurer pays its share of your costs.

HDHPs are managed care plans with lower premiums but much higher deductibles than other plans—a $1,250 minimum/$3,300 maximum for individual coverage, and a $2,500 minimum/$6,550 maximum for family coverage in 2014. There are also annual limits on what you must pay in out-of-pocket expenses—$6,350 for self-only and $12,700 for family coverage in 2014. Both sets of caps tend to increase slightly each year.

If you participate in an HDHP, you are entitled to open a **health savings account (HSA)** and contribute pretax income to pay for qualifying but uncovered medical expenses. Any amount you don't send one year can be rolled over to the following year.

INDIVIDUAL COVERAGE

You can purchase insurance either directly from an insurer or through a state, federal, or state-federal marketplace, or exchange, established under the ACA.

In most cases, you make two choices when you use an exchange, among providers and among four levels of coverage: bronze, silver, gold, and platinum. Each level covers a different percentage of your healthcare costs, from 60% with bronze to 90% with platinum. Prices vary as well, with the most comprehensive plans having the highest premiums. Plans with the lowest premiums tend to have very high deductibles.

Premium credits and cost-sharing subsidies are available to those who qualify, making the cost of buying coverage more affordable. This includes anyone whose income is up to 400% of the federal poverty line, which is about $90,000 for a family of four. In addition, there are limits to what you must pay in out of pocket expenses, similar to the out-of-pocket caps on HDHP plans. In some cases these limits may not apply until 2015.

For more information about ACA provisions, you can visit www.hhs.gov/Healthcare or www.healthcare.gov.

COBRA

If you leave a job where you've had health insurance, you may qualify for continued coverage under the Consolidated Omnibus Budget Reconciliation Act, better known as COBRA. It's not cheap—you normally pay 102% of your employer's cost—but it can be a good interim solution.

Investing

By investing, you move from planning to action.

When you invest, you buy things of value that you expect to increase your net worth and help you realize your goals by:

- Growing in value
- Providing income to reinvest or spend
- Producing both growth and income

Investing can be extremely rewarding if the average **return**, or earnings plus growth in value, on your investments is positive over time. But you always take some **risk** when you invest. For example, you could lose some, or even all, of your principal or earn less than you anticipate. This could mean you're not significantly better off than you were before investing.

You can improve your chances of investment success by learning as much as you can about how different investments work and choosing among them carefully. You can also benefit by investing strategically using **asset allocation** and **diversification**.

INVESTMENT BASICS

There are three core investment categories: **stocks, bonds**, and **cash**.

Each of these **asset classes** puts your money to work in a different way. The return on investment that they provide varies from class to class and from year to year. But over time all three types have provided positive results.

Stocks are ownership shares investors buy in a corporation

Bonds are loans investors make to corporations and governments

Cash equivalent investments include certificates of deposit (CDs) and US Treasury bills

MAKING INVESTMENTS

You can invest directly in individual stocks, bonds, and cash equivalents. You can invest in mutual funds, and exchange traded funds (ETFs) that own stocks, bonds, or cash equivalents.

You can open investment accounts with brokerage firms, mutual fund companies, banks, and insurance companies. And you may have the opportunity to invest through a retirement plan your employer offers. The assets you own in all these accounts make up your **investment portfolio**.

CHOOSING YOUR INVESTMENTS

Selecting investments that are right for you depends on your financial goals, specifically what you expect those goals to cost and when you want to achieve them. Among the things to consider in making your choices are the **return** you need, how much **risk** you're willing to take, and whether **liquidity** is a factor.

RETURN

What can you expect to earn on an investment?

While the return an asset class has provided in the past doesn't guarantee its future returns, understanding the historical performance of different classes lets you decide on how much emphasis to put on each class as you build your investment portfolio. Growth is generally associated with stocks and stock funds, income with bonds, and safety with FDIC-insured CDs.

What's the risk involved?

Investing always means taking some risks. To many people, the biggest risk is losing money, so they look for investments they consider safe. Usually that means putting money into bank CDs and US Treasury bills. The opposite but equally important risk is that your investments will not provide enough growth or income to offset the impact of inflation, the gradual increase in the cost of living. One solution may be choosing a variety of investments with different levels of risk.

LIQUIDITY

How accessible is your money?

If your investment money must be easily available to cover financial emergencies, you'll be concerned about **liquidity**, or how quickly it can be turned to cash with little or no loss of value. But when you invest for longer-term goals, liquidity is much less important. The most liquid investments, including CDs and Treasury bills, generally provide the lowest return but the most safety.

OTHER INVESTMENTS

You can find many other things to invest in, like options, commodities, real estate, or private partnerships, if you're looking for more variety or can afford to take added risks. But for most investors the basic three—stocks, bonds, and cash—should be the core of any investment portfolio. High on the list of reasons for that advice are the federal and state regulations that govern their sale and the fact that they trade in organized public markets, such as stock exchanges.

This means if you need to liquidate your assets, you can sell these investments easily, although not necessarily at a profit. Selling other types of investments may be slower or more difficult, if they don't trade in a public market.

WAYS TO INVEST

Just as there are different types of investments, there are different types of investment accounts.

You can put as much money as you wish in a **taxable** account each year and choose from a full menu of investments. You pay tax on any earnings your investments produce and on any gain in value from selling an investment for more than you paid to buy it. Qualifying dividends and long-term capital gains are taxed at a lower rate than your other income.

You may also have one or more **tax-deferred** retirement accounts. You can postpone taxes on investment earnings in a tax-deferred account until you withdraw. In some accounts you can also defer taxes on the amounts you invest. When you do withdraw, the tax that's due is figured at the same rate as you pay on other income. There are some limitations: The annual investment amount is often capped, and in some plans the investment menu may be limited. You may also owe a penalty if you withdraw early, which is usually before 59½.

Tax-exempt accounts are designed to help you pay for specific goals, such as retirement or education. If you follow the rules of the specific account you're using, no tax is due on any earnings in the account, either as they accumulate or when you withdraw. You do pay tax on the amounts you invest, and there may be limits on amounts you can invest each year.

Securities, by definition, are written proofs of ownership, like stock or bond certificates. But as electronic records have replaced paper, the term survives, to refer to the investments themselves.

Investment Risk

There's no such thing as a totally safe investment, but you can choose the level of risk you're comfortable with.

When you invest, you always take a certain amount of risk. The most dramatic consequence is the possibility you could lose some or all of your principal. But you also have to consider the more probable risk that you won't accumulate as much as you need to meet your retirement needs.

The two are interrelated. If you focus on reducing the risk of loss, you usually reduce your potential return and long-term financial security. If you can tolerate some fluctuation in your accounts' values, the most productive approach is often a middle ground, so that you include some investments with little risk to principal, a few with considerable risk, and the majority in assets that pose some risk but may also provide a strong return.

The bottom line is that you have to find the balance between too much and too little risk that fits your goals and your time horizon.

ESTIMATING RISK

There's no way to predict how investments will perform in the future or the risks that may limit their return. But by looking at the way that an investment or category of investment has performed in the past, you can get a sense of the level of return it's reasonable to expect.

For example, if the annual return on large-company stocks has averaged around 10% since 1926, it's unrealistic to assume that future returns will average 20% or more, despite the fact that they have been that high or higher in individual years. It's also true that they've been significantly lower—negative—in about one-third of the years.

KEEPING YOUR EYES CLOSED

One of the worst mistakes you can make as an investor is to ignore or underestimate the risks you're taking, or to assume nothing bad is going to happen. The only thing that's more risky is failing to invest because you're afraid you could lose money. Although you're likely to suffer some loss of portfolio value in a market downturn, in the next upturn you're positioned not only to regain lost ground but potentially to accumulate additional account value provided you stay invested.

THE INVESTMENT PYRAMID

Risk is the result of **volatility** — how much and how quickly the value of an investment changes — and **uncertainty**.

HIGHER RISK

Derivative products, such as futures contracts or some options, speculative equity investments, low-rated bonds, and certain commodities generally expose you to higher than average risk most of the time. In some cases, you could lose more than your initial investment.

MODERATE RISK

Some investments pose greater risk at some times than at others. Stocks, equity mutual funds, and ETFs, as a group, may provide strong returns in some but not all periods. Individual stocks can expose you to major gains or losses, based on a number of predictable and unpredictable factors. The same is true of bonds and real estate.

LIMITED RISK

Investing in the stocks and bonds of the largest and most stable issuers and the funds that invest in them poses more limited risk of major losses, but losses can and do occur in some periods. Even some investments considered essentially free of default risk, such as Treasury issues, can expose you to market risk.

LOWER RISK

The investments that pose the least risk of loss are insured bank products and short-term government issues. However, they typically expose you over the long term to inflation risk, which can be especially severe when interest rates are low.

VOLATILITY

Volatility refers to sudden and potentially dramatic changes in an investment's value. The more volatile an investment is, the greater the opportunity for a big profit within a short period. But there's also a greater potential for a major loss if the price drops and you sell for less than you paid to buy.

Some investments are inherently volatile, including derivatives whose value depends on the value of an underlying commodity, such as oil or wheat, and stock of new companies whose fortunes may change quickly based on an internal success or failure. Others may be volatile only when the investment markets in which they trade are in turmoil. Still others are rarely if ever volatile. For example, the market prices of high-rated bonds typically change slowly and within a limited range.

HIGHEST GAINS OR LOSSES
You can win big, but lose bigger, with risky investments.

One measure of a stock's volatility is its **beta**, which links its price movement to the average change in a control group of stocks. The less risk you prefer, the more likely you'll be to choose stocks with a beta lower than 1. Or, if you're seeking greater risk and greater potential return, you'll choose stocks with a beta higher than 1.

THE RISK OF HIGH YIELDS

One cardinal rule for successful investing is to know what you're doing. When the economy is down, and interest earnings decline, you might be tempted to seek an investment that produces the same high returns to which you've grown accustomed. The risk is buying lower-quality investments (which pay more to attract buyers), or investments you don't know anything about. It's a good idea to be skeptical of any investment described as risk free or that promises a dramatically higher yield than better-known products. Even if it's legitimate, it's likely to have strings attached.

LOWEST GAINS OR LOSSES
$10,000 in a savings account at rates below inflation will be safe but will lose value over time.

EMPLOYER STOCK

If you work for a publicly traded company, one of your retirement plan choices may be buying its stock. Or your employer may make its matching contributions in stock. There may be good reasons to choose the stock, including the fact that it gives you an opportunity to share in the success you're contributing to.

But there are risks in tying your financial security too tightly to a single source. At the worst, you could lose your job and your 401(k) could take a big hit. A useful guideline is to keep your holding to less than 20% of your account value.

OTHER KINDS OF RISK

Beyond the risks of the investments themselves—for example, a new company that fails or an established company that suffers severe losses—there are other risks you can't predict or control but must be prepared for:

MARKET RISK depends on the state of the economy as a whole. If the stock market tumbles, your stock investment will probably decline in value even if the companies whose stock you own are making money.

CURRENCY FLUCTUATION is increasingly a factor in investment risk, as more people put money into international markets. If the dollar rises in value, for example, the value of overseas investments declines — and vice versa.

INFLATION RISK affects the value of fixed-rate investments like bonds and CDs. If you buy when interest rates are low, the value of your investments declines as inflation and interest rates rise because the old interest rate isn't adjusted to keep pace.

POLITICAL TURMOIL is a risk because the economies of different nations are closely intertwined. Threats to the oil supply, for example, have disrupted the economy before and could again.

Figuring Your Return

Return is what you get back in relation to the amount you invest.

You start out as an investor by choosing investments. Then you need to monitor how your investments are performing and whether you're on track to meet your goals. As you evaluate your progress, you'll need to be prepared to make changes—by selling some investments and buying others—if certain ones aren't meeting your expectations.

As you monitor, though, you have to be realistic. If stocks in general are struggling to stay positive, as sometimes happens, you're can't expect the stocks or stock funds you own to provide a strong return. Selling them and substituting others isn't likely to improve performance if stocks are struggling. Nor will selling everything and putting what's left in a savings account.

By the same token, if the stock market is gaining value, you may want to consider replacing a stock whose return is still lagging. Another reason to replace a stock may be if the issuing company is in serious financial trouble from which it seems unlikely to emerge, and you want to avoid deeper losses.

DESIGNING THE TEST

The key to performance testing is **return on investment (ROI)**, or what you get back in relation to the amount you invest, called your investment **principal**.

If you start out with $1,000 and end up with $2,000, your return is $1,000 on that investment, or 100%. If a similar $1,000 investment grows to $1,500, your return is $500, or 50%—though of course you could also have a negative return in any period.

But unless you hold different investments for the same time period, you can't determine which has a stronger performance. What you need to compare your returns is the **annual percent return**, the average percentage that you've gained on each investment over a series of one-year periods.

For example, if you buy a share for $15 and sell it for $20, your profit is $5. If that happens within a year, your rate of return is an impressive 33% ($5÷$15=33.3%). If it takes five years, your average annual return will be closer to 7%, since the profit is spread over a five-year period.

Sell at	Profit	Return
Year 1	$5	33%
Year 3	$5	11%
Year 5	$5	6.6%

MEASURING TOTAL RETURN

In addition to the income on your investment, **total return** includes how much your investment gains or loses value measured by the change in its market price. For example, your total return on a stock is not just the dividends it pays, but how much you would gain or lose if you sold it.

Income +/– Change in value = Total return

You don't actually have to sell, or realize your gain or loss, to calculate total return. It's fine to figure it based on your unrealized gain. That's also known as a paper profit or a paper loss.

GETTING A GOOD RETURN

There's no absolute standard that qualifies a specific figure as a good return. The average return on specific classes of investments—small company stocks, for example—over a specific historical period are a matter of record. And total return figures for mutual fund performance are

CAPITAL GAINS AND LOSSES

Investments, including real estate, that you own are called **capital assets**. When you sell a capital asset at a higher price than you paid for it, the difference is a **capital gain**. If you sell at a lower price, you have a **capital loss**.

If you realize a capital gain after holding the investment for more than a year, it's a long-term gain. But if you realize the gain within a year or less, it's a short-term gain.

Long-term gains are taxed at a lower rate than your regular income, which is also the rate you pay on short-term gains. So if you can wait to sell until the year has passed, you improve your investment income by reducing the tax you owe.

reported regularly. You can compare how well your investments are doing against those numbers as a starting point.

Another factor to take into account when evaluating return is the current inflation rate. Your return needs to be higher than the inflation rate if your investments are going to increase in value. In fact, **real return** is market return minus the inflation rate.

FIGURING RETURN IS NOT THAT SIMPLE

Figuring out the actual return on your investments can be difficult because:

- The amount of your investment changes. Most investment portfolios are active, with money moving in and out
- The method of computing return can vary. For example, performance can be **averaged** or **compounded**, which changes the rate of return dramatically, as the chart below demonstrates
- The time you hold specific investments varies. **When** you buy or sell can have a dramatic effect on overall return
- The return on some investments — like limited partnerships or real estate investments — is difficult to pin down, partly because they're not publicly traded. You have to evaluate them by different standards than you do stocks or bonds, including their tax advantages

COMPOUND VS. AVERAGE RATE OF RETURN

Here are six sets of investment returns totaling 27% over three years. While the average annualized return in each case is 9%, compound annual returns vary significantly. The most volatile investment, number 6, provided the weakest compound return despite having the highest one year return, at 40%, in part because it also had the lowest, or 5%, and that loss occured in the first year.

Investment	1	2	3	4	5	6
Year 1	9%	5%	0%	0%	-1%	-5%
Year 2	9%	10%	7%	0%	-1%	8%
Year 3	9%	12%	20%	27%	29%	40%
Average return	9.00%	9.00%	9.00%	9.00%	9.00%	9.00%
Compound return	9.00%	8.96%	8.69%	8.29%	8.13%	6.96%

USING BENCHMARKS

One of things you'll want to know as you evaluate performance is how well your investments are doing currently in comparison with other investments that have similar characteristics and return potential—two large US corporations, for example, or two telecommunications companies. That's where **benchmarks** help.

A benchmark is an index or average that reflects the changing value of a particular financial market or part of a market, called a sector. The benchmark serves as a standard against which to compare the performance of an investment that is part of that market or sector.

For example, the Standard & Poor's 500 Index (S&P 500) tracks the performance of 500 large, widely held US companies. It's the benchmark for large-company US stocks and the mutual funds and ETFs that invest in those stocks. Other benchmarks track small companies, long-term government bonds, types of mutual funds, and every other market segment you can imagine in the United States and around the world—including telecommunications companies.

Comparison with a benchmark provides relevant information, however, only when the investment belongs within the segment of the market that the benchmark tracks. You can usually find a list of relevant benchmarks by visiting the website of a company in which you're interested.

Asset Allocation

Asset allocation is a strategy for building and managing your investment portfolio.

An **asset class** is a group of investments that shares specific characteristics that differentiate it from other groups of investments. Among the primary distinctions are that each asset class puts your money to work in a different way than the others and exposes you to different types of investment risk.

Asset allocation means dividing your investment portfolio among asset classes—primarily stocks, bonds, and cash equivalents, but potentially tangible property including real estate and precious metals, and derivatives, including options and futures contracts. Stocks—also called equities—include stock mutual funds and exchange traded funds (ETFs) that track stock indexes. Bonds include bond mutual funds and ETFs that track bond indexes. Cash equivalents include certificates of deposit (CDs), US Treasury bills, and money market mutual funds.

Generally you allocate on a percentage basis, assigning part of your investment principal to each asset class you're using. For example, you might invest 60% in one class, 20% in a second, and 20% in a third. Or you might allocate one-third of the total to each of three classes.

LOOKING FOR RESULTS

Your allocation typically has a major impact on your investment **return**. That's because no single asset class consistently produces the best return every year, based on a number of factors including what's happening in the investment markets and in the economy at large. And a class that has been strong one year may be weak the next.

If you were invested primarily in the class that was outperforming the others in a particular year, your increased portfolio value would reflect those gains. But if in the following year or two that class underperformed, your portfolio value would be dragged down by the losses. The challenge is that while this up-and-down pattern repeats regularly, the timing is not predictable.

Remember, too, that while asset allocation can help you manage risk, it doesn't guarantee a profit or prevent a loss in a falling market.

MANAGING RISK

Although each asset class is made up of many different securities, certain recurring market conditions affect an entire asset class in a relatively predictable way. For example, if interest rates are low and

ALLOCATION

An asset allocation model is a blueprint for spreading your investment capital among different asset classes. The most suitable model varies, based on

AGGRESSIVE

An **aggressive** allocation, which may be appropriate for young people or those with a steady source of fixed income, tends to emphasize equities, with as much as 80% to 90% of the portfolio being invested in stock, stock mutual funds, and stock ETFs.

HOW ALLOCATION WORKS

Once you have chosen an appropriate allocation—say that you decide to put 60% of your assets into stock, 30% into bonds, and 10% into cash—the next step is to put it into practice. For example, you might have $1,000 to invest. You'd use $600 to buy shares of a stock fund, put $300 in a bond fund, and place the remaining $100 in a savings account. The next time you have $1,000 to invest, you do the same thing. And, if you rolled over $10,000 from a 401(k) to an individual retirement account (IRA), $6,000 would go into stock funds, $3,000 into bond funds and other fixed-income alternatives, and $1,000 into cash equivalents, such as US Treasury bills (T-bills) or a short-term bond fund.

corporate earnings are strong, stocks as a group have tended to produce robust returns while bond returns were likely to be more anemic. This is known as **systemic risk**.

By creating a portfolio of asset classes that respond differently to particular market and economic conditions—not all of which are likely to occur at the same time—you have a better chance of weathering some major losses without significantly reducing your potential for long-term growth. That's because gains in one asset class can not only offset losses in another, but, if they're strong enough, can also provide a positive return for the year.

Asset classes that produce their strongest returns in different economic climates are described as having a low or negative **correlation**. In other words, they don't respond the same way to a particular stimulus. For example, stocks and cash equivalents tend to have a very low correlation. When the interest rate on T-bills is high, stock returns tend to be limited or even negative.

MODELS

an investor's age, economic situation, and tolerance for investment risk, plus expectations about how the market is likely to perform.

Comparing different ways to allocate may help you determine the model that might be best for you.

MODERATE

A **moderate** allocation might assign between 50% and 70% of the total to equities, depending on your age, your financial goals, and your other financial resources, with the balance going to fixed income and some cash.

CONSERVATIVE

A **conservative** allocation, which may be appropriate for older people wanting to preserve capital and collect regular income, might assign 40% of the total to equities, with the rest divided between bonds and cash, depending on the economy and an investor's personal financial situation.

A TIME TO REALLOCATE

Over time, you may want to modify your portfolio allocation in response to a number of different situations.

As you get closer to retirement, you may want to shift some of your assets out of potentially volatile growth investments, such as stock or stock funds, into income-producing investments that have tended to be more stable in value.

You may want to reallocate your portfolio in response to major life events that have an impact on your financial situation, such as getting married or divorced, having children, or changing jobs.

ALLOCATION CHOICES

Stock has historically provided the strongest return by doing well in some years, even though results have been flat or lost ground in others.

Bonds have produced strong returns in some years and weaker returns in others, though the highs and lows tend to be less extreme than with stock.

Cash equivalents usually provide the smallest, but most consistent, returns.

Real estate tends to increase in value over time, sometimes dramatically. It can lose value, too, and real estate is illiquid, which means it may be hard to sell easily at the price you want.

Diversification

Diversifying means buying a number of investments within an asset class.

No matter how good a recipe is, it doesn't guarantee high-quality results. You also need superior ingredients. In investment terms, this means building your portfolio by selecting a diversified group of securities for each asset class you invest in and ensuring that each security meets your criteria for investing.

For example, if US equities is one of your asset classes, you might choose a number of **individual stocks**. Or you might diversify by choosing a variety of **mutual funds** or **exchange traded funds (ETFs)** investing in US equities.

Diversification within each asset class is essential because it allows you to offset, or dilute, security-specific risks.

FINER DISTINCTIONS

Most asset classes are defined in fairly sweeping terms, such as US equities or long-term US debt. There are more than 4,500 listed common stocks that belong to the first category, several thousand that aren't listed, and more than 500 ETFs and 4,500 mutual funds that invest in stocks. Long-term US debt includes several million corporate, federal government, and municipal issues.

Subclasses, or smaller categories, within the broad classes typically behave differently from each other even though they share the essential defining features of the class to which they belong.

For example, companies issuing equities can be divided by **market capitalization** into large, mid, small, and micro subclasses. Differences in capitalization generally indicate differences in growth potential, share-price volatility, and the likelihood that the issuing company will survive an economic downturn.

Other ways to distinguish equity subclasses are by industry, sector, and valuation—that is, whether they're overpriced or underpriced based on a criterion such as average price/earnings ratio (P/E) for their peers, as well as domestic and international issues.

On the fixed-income side, differentiators include taxable and tax-free status, interest rate, term, callability, and rating.

NOT PEAS IN A POD

You can expect securities that share defining characteristics to react in much the same way to specific factors or situations. For example, one of the major determinants of the value of any long-term corporate bond is its credit rating. With a downgrade, its value drops, and with an upgrade, its value increases.

As another example, one of the key factors that affects the value of a stock is the quality of the company's management. Some companies have exceptional management and, as a result, tend to outperform their peers. Other companies have inferior management and tend to falter even though they may be producing comparable products or providing similar services.

These are examples of a **security-specific risk**, or, in the language of asset allocation, **nonsystemic risk**.

LIMITING YOUR EXPOSURE

The possibility of a downgrade in a long-term corporate bond's rating that dramatically reduces a bond's return represents a significant source of risk. Compounding the problem, it's hard to predict when the credit quality of a particular bond will change. While this risk

A WORD OF WARNING

In addition to managing nonsystemic risk, one of the goals of creating a diversified portfolio is to provide a more consistent return. But while diversification can help you manage risk, it doesn't guarantee a profit or prevent a loss in a falling market.

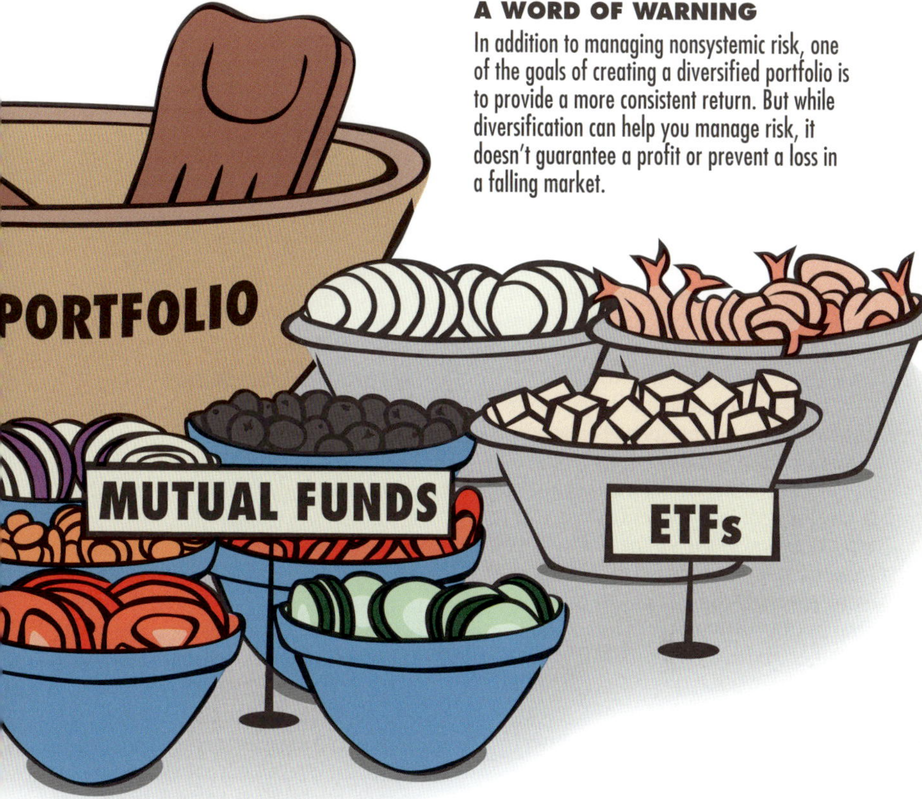

is significant with any single bond, you can reduce your overall risk by buying an assortment of similar bonds.

If, for instance, instead of owning one bond you own a diversified portfolio of bonds, then the credit quality of some of the bonds may be upgraded while the credit quality of others is downgraded. Over time, the upgrades and downgrades may equalize so that, overall, the impact of credit changes on your portfolio's return is reduced. In other words, a certain amount of credit risk can be diversified away.

As an investor, it's often hard to know which companies are well-managed and which are poorly managed—except in hindsight. However, in a diversified portfolio of stocks, the effects of superior and inferior management tend to balance out. Therefore the impact of management quality is another nonsystemic risk that you can reduce or even eliminate through diversification.

But adding investments randomly is unlikely to achieve the diversification you seek. The quality and range of investments and the care with which they're selected is more important than how many you own.

DIVERSIFYING WITH FUNDS

A well-diversified portfolio is likely to contain securities from various subclasses—though not necessarily from all of them—within each of its asset classes.

For example, short-term bonds, which mature in less than a year, tend to be less vulnerable to inflation risk than bonds with 30-year terms. They're also much less likely to expose you to credit risk since the issuer's ability to pay will not be subject to as many changing factors. But in most environments they pay lower rates.

One approach to consider is concentrating your investment assets in mutual funds and ETFs. Because each fund is diversified in its own right, you don't have the responsibility of choosing individual investments or concerns about owning enough different securities in any category. And because you can choose among a broad range of funds, each of which invests to meet a particular objective, you can create a diversified portfolio of diversified funds.

But as part of your selection process, you'll want to evaluate the fees and other costs of owning the funds you're considering. The higher the annual expenses, the lower the return you realize.

Investing in Stocks

Stocks are ownership shares, or equity, in a corporation.

When you buy stock in a corporation, you become one of its owners. If the company does well, you may receive part of its profits as dividends and see the price of your stock increase. But if the company fares badly, the value of your investment can drop, sometimes substantially.

A stock has no absolute value. At any given time, its value depends on whether the shareholders want to hold it or sell it, and on what other investors are willing to pay for it. If lots of people want shares, the stock's value will go up. If a company is losing money or a particular industry is doing poorly, those stocks will probably drop in value. Some stocks are undervalued, which means they sell for less than analysts think they're worth, while others are overvalued.

Investors' attitudes are determined by several factors: whether or not they expect to make money with the stock, current stock market conditions, and the overall state of the economy.

INVESTOR CONCERNS

Some people hesitate to invest in the stock market because they consider it too risky. Afraid of choosing the wrong stock or being battered in a crash, they prefer to stick with investments they consider safe.

The problem with that approach is that by skipping stocks, investors are missing out on a reliable source of long-term gains. While you can always lose money in a single year or on a single stock, investors who have held a portfolio of stocks through any 15-year period since 1926 have always come out ahead.

Usually, the greater danger is not sticking with stocks. Investors who sell their shares when the market drops, rather than riding out the downturn, are more likely to lose money than people who leave their portfolios alone, or those who buy additional shares when prices are depressed.

THE WORLD OF STOCKS

Stocks as an asset class are all alike in providing the opportunity to own shares in the issuing company and prosper if the company prospers. But within the overall class, stocks can be categorized in a number of ways that differentiate them from the others.

For example, some stocks are **listed** on an organized market, such as the New York Stock Exchange (NYSE) or the NASDAQ Stock Market. Others trade **over-the-counter (OTC)**. One advantage of investing in listed stocks are that they tend to be more liquid, so you can sell when you wish, though not always at the price you'd like. There's also generally more information available about listed stocks, which you can use to make an informed investment decision.

Stocks can also be categorized by the size of the issuing company, or what's known as **market capitalization**, or market cap. You find market cap by multiplying the number of outstanding shares by the current price of a share. Outstanding shares are those that investors own.

The largest companies, called **large caps**, include some of the oldest and best known US businesses as well as a number of newer powerhouses, many of them technology companies. Large cap prices tend to be less volatile than those of **small-caps** or **mid-caps**. They are also more likely to pay dividends than smaller, often newer, companies.

Smaller companies may provide more growth in value as they expand. But they may be less resilient in tough times because they have fewer financial resources. Mid-caps share some characteristics of the other two: greater growth potential on the one hand but also less financial depth.

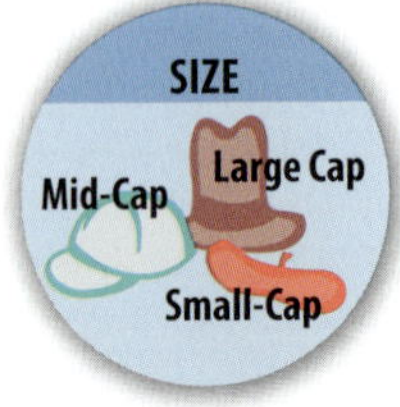

HOW DO INVESTORS MAKE MONEY?

Investors buy stock to make money:

1. **Through dividend payments while they own the stock**
2. **By selling the stock for more than they paid to buy**

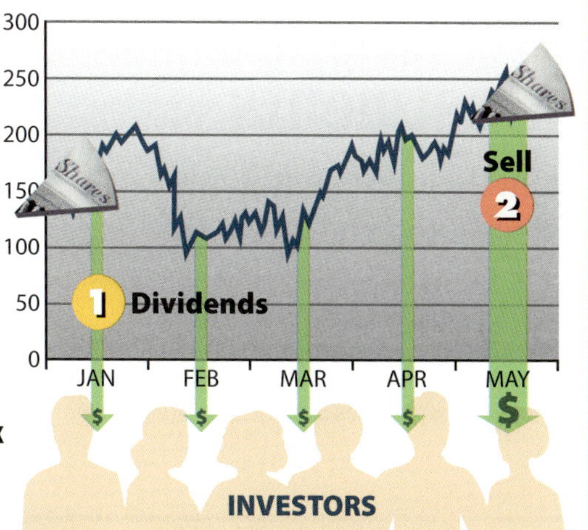

FINDING P/E

A stock's **price-to-earnings (P/E) ratio** is one tool investors use to evaluate a stock's current price in relation to its potential for longer-term success. If the P/E varies substantially from the market's average P/E, it's wise to try to understand why. A very high P/E may be the result of great promise or irrational enthusiasm, while very low P/E may be the sign of hidden potential or imminent collapse. That's why P/E can never be the only indicator you check.

Another way stocks differ is how they perform in different economic environments. Stocks described as **cyclical** tend to flourish when the economy is strong and suffer when it weakens. Airlines, the hospitality industry, and other providers of nice-to-have but not essential goods and services tend to be cyclical. **Defensive** stocks, on the other hand, are often more resilient in recessionary periods because demand for their products and services continues. Utility, pharmaceutical, and healthcare companies are examples.

A further way to differentiate is between **growth** and **value**. Growth stocks are shares in companies that reinvest most of their profits to expand and strengthen their business. Value stocks are trading at a lower price than would seem appropriate based on their assets and market potential. That may be the case if the company has had financial problems or if it is part of an industry that is out of favor with investors.

BUILDING A STOCK PORTFOLIO

A smart approach to investing in stocks is to create a diversified portfolio, with:

- Some domestic stocks, whose issuers are based in the United States, and some international stocks, whose issuers are based in other countries
- Stocks with different market caps
- Cyclical as well as defensive stocks
- Both growth and value stocks, as well as dividend-paying stocks that provide regular income

KEEPING TRACK

Your brokerage firm creates a regular monthly or quarterly statement reporting your current account value and detailing all transactions in your account during the period, including dividend or interest payments, purchases and sales, and any cash infusions or withdrawals. The firm also provides a confirmation for each trade, including the price and commission.

It's smart to review these documents to track how your portfolio is doing. Additionally, they can provide a heads-up to potential problems: unauthorized trades, for example, or unexplained fees and charges.

BUY AND WATCH

When some investors choose a stock, they keep it through thick and thin, a strategy known as **buy and hold**. Other investors buy and sell more frequently, which means they select stocks they think are going to increase rapidly in value. When the price goes up a certain percent — 15% to 20% for example — they sell and buy something else.

Both approaches work. What works less well is ignoring your portfolio. If you don't pay attention to how your stocks are doing, you could be keeping some that aren't living up to the expectations you had for them when you invested. It happens to everybody. The best solution is to sell your losers and identify new investments that have the potential to make your portfolio stronger.

Taking Stock of Your Investments

To invest intelligently, and to track how well you're doing, you have to understand the language of stocks.

You can find current data on any stock in your portfolio or on a stock you may want to purchase on the company's website as well as newspaper sites and finance sites.

You can request regular updates on specific stocks or track an online portfolio, which may, but doesn't have to, mirror the portfolio you actually own.

Caterpillar Inc. (CAT) - NYSE

84.14 ↑1.20(1.44%) 2:08PM EDT - Nasdaq Real

Prev Close:	82.94	Day's Range:
Open:	83.41	52wk Range:
Bid:	84.11 x 100	Volume:
Ask:	84.13 x 200	Market Cap:
Beta:	1.88	P/E (ttm):
		EPS (ttm):
		Div & Yield:

Close tells you a stock's closing price for the previous day. Usually the daily differences are small even if the 52-week spread is large.

Bid is the highest price a buyer offers, and **ask** is the lowest price that a seller wants. The difference between them is the spread. Bid and ask are in constant play throughout the trading day.

Highest and lowest prices of each stock are shown for the last 52 weeks. The range between the prices is a measure of the stock's **volatility**. The more volatile a stock is, the more you can make or lose within a relatively short investment period. The percentage of change is more significant than the dollar amount: a $5 change from $5 to $10, a 100% change, shows more volatility than a $5 change from $30 to $35, a 17% change.

Earnings per share (EPS) is one measure of the company's health. Investors see improved earnings per share as a sign of increasing profitability, especially when there is a pattern of gains over several quarters or years.

Price/Earnings ratio shows the relationship between a stock's price and the company's earnings for the past four quarters. It's figured by dividing the current price per share by the earnings per share.

There is no ideal P/E ratio. A stock with a low P/E ratio — say 10 — may seem like a bargain. But the company could have problems that will hurt future earnings.

Meanwhile, a stock with a high P/E — say 37 or more — may seem overpriced. But it could be growing so fast that its future earnings will be much higher, justifying the price.

BULLS AND BEARS
Individual stocks and the stock market as a whole gain and lose value in recurring cycles of growth and decline. Periods of growth are identified as **bull markets**. Periods when prices drop 20% or more from their most recent high are known as **bear markets**. The time that elapses from the start of one bull market to the start of the next one, including the bear market phase, is known as a **full market cycle**.

Within any phase of a market cycle, the prices of individual stocks or the market as a whole can change direction for a time, rising in a bear market or falling in a bull market, before reverting to the dominant trend. If prices drop in the 10% range, it's described as a **correction**. But a correction is just that. It doesn't necessarily signal the beginning of a bear market.

The chief unknown with market cycles is how long the separate phases will last, which could be months or years.

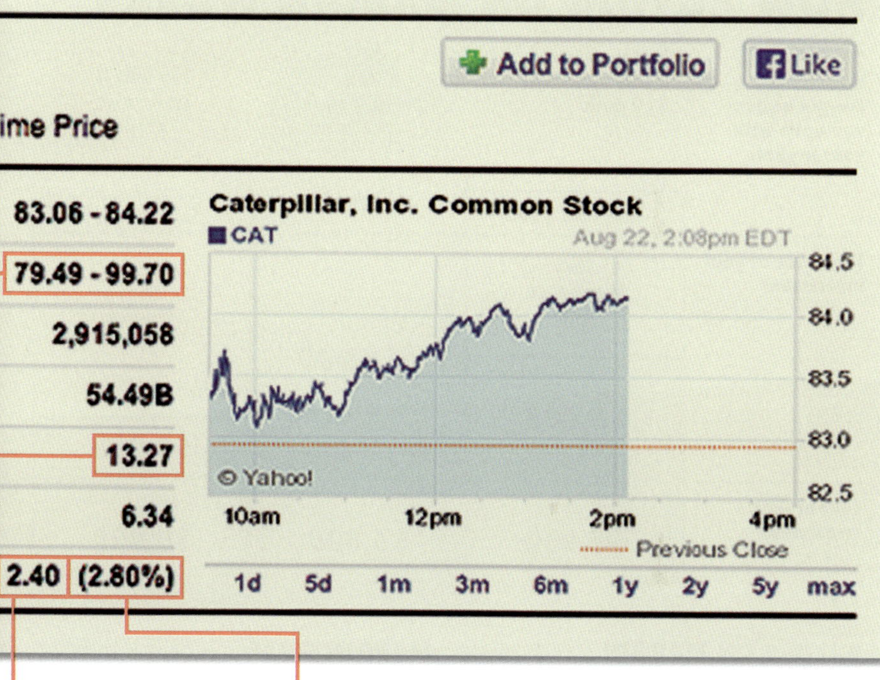

While P/E ratios can help you evaluate a stock, P/E is not the only factor to consider.

Cash dividend per share is an estimate of the anticipated yearly dividend per share in dollars and cents. Sometimes the prices of stocks that pay dividends are less volatile than the prices of stocks with no dividend. Caterpillar's yearly dividend is estimated at $2.40 per share. If you owned 100 shares, you'd receive $240 in dividend payments, probably in quarterly payments of $60. Preferred stocks tend to pay higher dividends.

Percent yield tells you the percentage of a stock's price paid as a dividend. Here, the yield of 2.8% means the annual per share dividend of $2.40 is equal to 2.8% of the price.

Yield provides only a partial picture. Sometimes the yield can look very attractive — say 10% — because price of the stock has fallen but management hasn't adjusted the dividend downward. And some companies choose not to pay a dividend, preferring to reinvest profits in new products or factories, which may result in higher profits later.

ONLINE ALTERNATIVES
You can find current trading information — sometimes in real time but more often with a 15 or 20 minute delay — on market websites including the New York Stock Exchange (www.nyse.com), and the Nasdaq Stock Market (www.nasdaq.com) as well as on brokerage firm and news company websites. Many financial publishers will customize a newsletter tailored to your specific interests, such as late-breaking news on the stocks in your portfolio or those you are following.

Other Ways to Trade

Some stock investors use leverage to increase gains, but they risk magnifying losses.

Experienced investors sometimes buy stocks on margin or sell stocks short, two techniques that can boost profits though they may also result in losses. The profits occur when you anticipate correctly what a stock will cost in the future, and the losses result from getting the direction wrong or having to wait a long time for the anticipated change to occur. Like other leveraged investments, for which you borrow part of the cost, you must repay the loan regardless of how the deal turns out.

HOW BUYING ON MARGIN WORKS

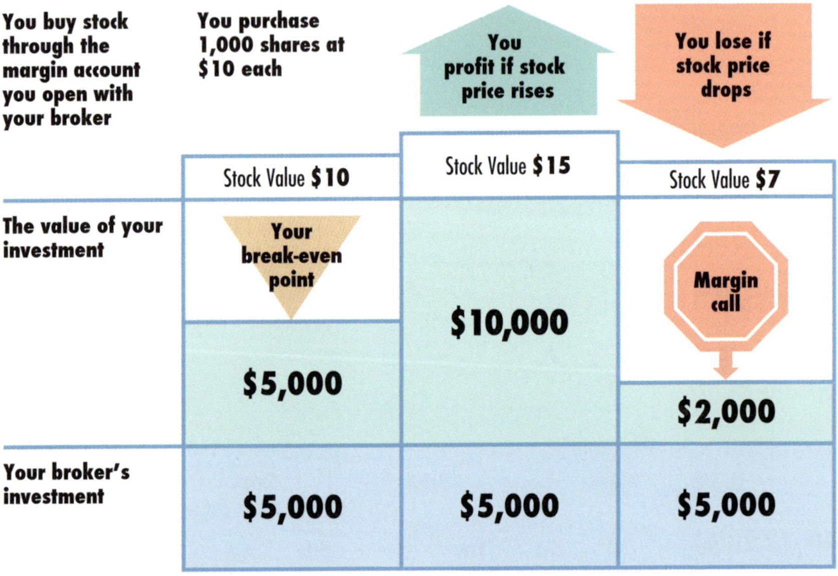

You buy stock through the margin account you open with your broker

You purchase 1,000 shares at $10 each

You profit if stock price rises

You lose if stock price drops

	Stock Value $10	Stock Value $15	Stock Value $7
The value of your investment	Your break-even point $5,000	$10,000	Margin call $2,000
Your broker's investment	$5,000	$5,000	$5,000

BUYING ON MARGIN

To **buy on margin**, you must open a margin account with your broker and deposit the required minimum, often $2,000, in cash or marketable securities. That gives you the right to borrow up to 50% of the purchase price of a stock you buy through the account.

For example, if you buy 1,000 shares of a stock at $10 a share, you would use $5,000 of your own money and borrow the balance. If the price goes up to $15 a share, you can sell, repay the $5,000 you borrowed, and realize a profit of $5,000, or 100%, minus commissions and interest. If you invested just your $5,000 to buy 500 shares, you'd have just half the gain—$2,500 or 50%—before commissions but owe no interest.

The risk, however, is that the price could stay flat or fall. If it dropped to $7 a share, and you sold to prevent further losses, you'd absorb the total $3,000 loss because you'd still owe your broker $5,000.

MARGIN CALLS

Brokers protect themselves against losses by issuing a **margin call** if the value of an investment purchased through a margin account falls below a specified percentage—never less than 25% and often 30% or higher. The call requires you to deposit additional cash or securities to bring your equity up to the required level. If you can't afford to, or don't, **meet the call**, your broker can sell securities in your account to cover the shortfall. In the example here, if your broker required 30%, you'd have to add $100 to bring your equity to $2,100, or 30% of $7,000.

BUYING RIGHTS

Companies sometimes offer their stockholders the opportunity to buy more shares below market price during a limited time period. These written offers, called rights, are actively traded in many stock markets around the world.

PROFESSIONAL ANALYSIS

Professional stock analysts use different methods to evaluate a stock's prospects and decide which ones they will advise investors to buy or sell.

Fundamental analysts concentrate on the economic health—the balance sheet and income statements—of individual companies, and on their management and their position in the industry, in order to forecast a stock's future performance.

Technical analysts use past price patterns to predict how individual companies, industries, or the market as a whole will do in the future. These analysts use charts or computer programs to identify and project price trends, usually in the short term.

Many investors use a combination of fundamental and technical analysis, the former to decide what to buy and the latter to decide when to buy it.

HOW SELLING SHORT WORKS

You borrow 100 shares from your broker

You sell the 100 shares at the $10 price, getting $1,000

You profit if stock price drops

You lose if stock price rises

	Stock Value **$10**	Stock Value **$7.50**	Stock Value **$12.50**
Shares you owe your broker	**100** Shares	**100** Shares	**100** Shares
Your cost to pay back the shares		**$750**	**$1,250**
Your profit—or loss before interest and other fees		**$250** Profit	**$250** Loss

SELLING SHORT

Selling short is selling a stock before you buy it because you think the price is going down. To sell short, you use a **margin account**, and borrow stock you don't own from your broker. Ideally, when the price drops, you **cover your short position** by buying the stock for less than you sold it for. You give the stock to your broker to replace the shares you borrowed and pocket your profit.

For example, if you sell short 100 shares at $10 a share, the price drops and you buy 100 shares two weeks later for $7.50 a share, you make $2.50 profit per share (minus the interest and commission you owe your broker). That's approximately a 33% return.

The risk is that the price of the stock might go up instead of down. Then you may have to cover your short position by paying more for the stock than you sold it for, so you could potentially lose more than the amount you invested.

WHAT ARE WARRANTS?

When you buy a **warrant**, you pay a small price now for the right to buy a certain number of shares at a fixed price during a specified period in the future. For example, you might pay $1 a share for the right to buy the stock at $8 within five years. If you **exercise**, or use, your warrant when the selling price is $12, you'll be $3 ahead ($12 – ($8 + $1) = $3).

If the price of the stock is below the **exercise price** when the warrant expires, the warrant is worthless. But before it expires, the warrant can increase in value if the stock price rises. So it's important to keep track of the underlying stock during a warrant's life span so you can exercise or sell if it makes financial sense.

Warrants are sold by companies that plan to issue stock, or by those that want to raise cash by selling stocks they hold in reserve. Once a warrant is offered, it has a life of its own, and can be bought and sold as well as exercised.

Investing in Bonds

Bonds attract investors because they usually pay regular interest income and pledge to repay principal.

Bonds are loans you make to corporations or governments. Unlike buying stocks or **equity** securities, which makes you a part owner, buying bonds, or **debt** securities, makes you a creditor.

Bonds are called fixed-income securities because they pay interest at a specific rate for a specific term, from a year or less to 30 years or more. The longer the term, the higher the interest rate generally is, though the difference is not always significant. When the term ends, the bond matures, and the issuer repays par value. If not, the issuer is in default and investors generally lose at least some principal.

TYPES OF BONDS

Type	Description	Features
Corporate Bonds	Bonds are the major source of corporate borrowing. **Debentures** are backed by the general credit of the corporation. **Asset-backed bonds** are backed by specific corporate assets like property or equipment.	• Sold through brokers • Interest is taxable • Top-rated bonds pose limited risk of default • Higher yield than government bonds with similar terms • Sold in $1,000 units
Municipal Bonds	Millions of bonds have been issued by state and local governments. **General obligation** bonds are backed by the full faith and credit of the issuer, and **revenue bonds** by the earnings of the particular project being financed.	• Sold through brokers • Pay lower interest rates than comparably rated corporate bonds and US Treasurys • Tax-exempt interest • Sold in $1,000 units
US Treasury Bonds	Intermediate (2, 3, 5, 7,and 10 years) term government notes are a major source of government funding. Long-term (30 year) government bonds also fund government operations.	• Sold through TreasuryDirect or brokers • Highest credit quality • Inflation-indexed bonds (TIPS) offer income protection • Sold in $100 units
US Treasury Bills	Largest components of the money market, where short-term (4, 13, 26, and 52 week) securities are bought and sold. Investors use T-bills for part of their cash reserve or as an interim holding place. Interest is the difference between the discounted buying price and the amount paid at maturity.	• Sold through TreasuryDirect or brokers • Essentially free of credit and market risk • Discount rate set at auction • Interest taxable at federal but not state and local levels • Sold in $100 units
Agency Bonds	Federal, state and local agencies sell bonds. The best known are federally guaranteed mortgage-backed bonds sold by Ginnie Mae (Government National Mortgage Association).	• Sold directly through banks, or by brokers • Marginally higher risk and higher interest than Treasury bonds • May require investment of $25,000

US savings bonds are often the first investment people own, whether they were a gift or purchased with payroll deductions. Unlike other Treasury issues or municipal and corporate bonds, savings bonds aren't marketable and can't be bought and sold among investors. Instead, owners hold the bonds for up to 30 years before redeeming them for the principal plus interest.

Interest accrues monthly and is paid at redemption, though three months interest is withheld as a penalty on any savings bond that has not been held at least five years.

Paper bonds that were issued before 2012 can be redeemed or converted to electronic form using a program called Smart Exchange or held until redemption. The five-year penalty period doesn't apply to conversions, and no income tax is due on converted amounts.

TREASURY ISSUES

High-quality, or **investment-grade**, bonds are considered conservative investments because you're likely to receive regular interest payments plus the bond's face value, or **par**, when it matures.

Treasury bonds, notes, and **bills** are considered essentially free of default risk. They are backed by the "full faith and credit" of the government, which has the power to tax its citizens to pay its debts. Corporate and municipal bonds are rated by independent rating services—the best known are Standard & Poor's, Moody's, and Fitch—which provide an opinion about the financial stability of the issuer and assign a rating—from AAA (or Aaa) to D. Any bond rated Baa or higher by Moody's, or BBB or higher by Standard & Poor's, is considered investment quality. Usually, the higher a bond's rating, the lower the interest it must pay to attract buyers.

AVOIDING COMMISSIONS

The least expensive way to buy and sell US Treasury issues is without commission through the federal system called **TreasuryDirect**. You set up an account and buy or reinvest online at www.treasurydirect.gov. The system deposits your interest and principal electronically in your linked bank account, and debits the account for new purchases.

WHAT ARE JUNK BONDS?
Investors willing to take risks for higher yields buy corporate or municipal bonds with low ratings—or no ratings at all—commonly known as junk bonds.

The current interest rate at Treasury auctions and the price of the 30-year bond in the secondary market are considered benchmarks of investor attitudes toward the economy.

SAVINGS BONDS: TRIED, AND TRUE

You can buy US savings bonds—up to $10,000 per person a year—through a TreasuryDirect account.

- Series EE bonds pay a fixed rate of return, determined by purchase date, for 30 years
- Series I bonds pay inflation-adjusted interest for 30 years
- You can invest as little as $25
- There's no commission, and no state or local tax on the interest, and you don't owe federal taxes until you redeem the bond

You may qualify to avoid taxes entirely if you use the bonds to pay for your child's education.

INFLATION PROTECTION
One risk of buying most bonds is that the income you earn is fixed for the term of the loan. But if you buy inflation-indexed US Treasury notes (TIPS), your principal is increased as inflation rises. That lets you maintain the buying power provided by the fixed-income portion of your investment portfolio. But the principal also could decrease if inflation drops.

The Value of Bonds

Some of the factors to consider in evaluating bonds as potential investments are the purchase price, the interest rate, and the yield.

If you buy a bond at face value, or **par**, when it is issued and hold it until it matures, you'll earn interest at the stated, or **coupon**, rate. For example, if you buy a 20-year $1,000 bond paying 5%, you'll earn $50 a year for 20 years. The **yield**, or your return on investment, will also be 5%. And you get your $1,000 back.

You can also buy and sell bonds through a broker after their date of issue. This is known as the **secondary**, or resale, market. There the price fluctuates, with a bond sometimes selling at more than par value, or at a **premium**, and sometimes below, at a **discount**.

Changes in price are directly tied to the interest rate of the bond. If its rate is higher than the rate being paid on similar bonds, buyers are willing to pay more than par to get the higher interest. But if its rate is lower, the bond will sell for less than par. The higher the price you pay, the lower the yield, or what you earn on your investment. Similarly, when the price is below par, the yield is up.

UNDERSTANDING BOND PRICES

Corporate and municipal bonds are priced in decimals, as stocks are, with a par value of $1,000 as the base. A bond trading at 101.250 sells for $1,012.50 while one trading at 99.291 sells for $992.91. While many bonds move very little above or below par, investor demand for a particular issue may drive its price substantially higher. Similarly, if investors are selling a particular issue, perhaps because its rating has been cut, its price may fall well below $1,000.

You can find information for the most actively traded investment grade, high yield, and convertible bonds by checking FINRA TRACE at www.finra.org. TRACE is an acronym for Trade Reporting and Compliance Engine.

For comparable information about municipal bonds, check the EMMA website of the Municipal Securities Rulemaking Board (MSRB) at www.emma.msrb.org. EMMA is an acronym for Electronic Municipal Market Access.

US Treasury issues are also priced in decimals, but the par value of each bond, note, or bill is $100 rather than $1,000. You can check for the latest data at TreasuryDirect.gov.

FIGURING CURRENT YIELD ON BONDS

If you pay a premium for a bond, in the secondary market you still earn the same interest that was paid when the bond was issued at par. But since you paid more, the **current yield** — or the percentage of your investment — is less.

For example, if you bought a bond with a par value of $1,000 and a 5% interest rate for $1,040, the current yield would be 4.8%.

$$\frac{\$50 \text{ Interest}}{\$1{,}040 \text{ Current market price}} = 4.8\% \text{ Current yield}$$

HOW YIELD CHANGES

Yield from a $1,000 bond with an interest rate of 5%	Interest payment	Yield
If you buy it at par value of $1,000:	$50.00	**5%**
If you buy it at a discount price of $800:	$50.00	**6.25%**
If you buy it at a premium price of $1,200:	$50.00	**4.17%**

WHAT IS YIELD TO MATURITY?

The way to evaluate your return on a secondary market bond is its **yield to maturity**. This calculation is based on the interest payments you'll receive until the time it matures and what you pay for the bond, above or below its par value. Your broker can tell you a bond's yield to maturity or you can check online resources, including www.finra.org or www.emma.mrsb.org.

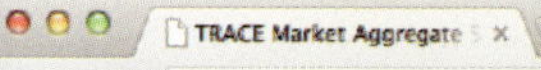

FINRA TRACE Corporate Bond Data

Most Active Investment Grade Bonds

Issuer Name	Coupon	Maturity	Rating Moody's/ S&P	Last	Change	Yield %
MORGAN STANLEY	2.125%	Apr 2018	Baa1/A–/A	98.893	0.683	2.374
LYONDELLBASELL INDS N V	5.000%	Apr 2019	Baa2//	110.556	–0.010	2.883
BANK AMER CORP	6.000%	Sept 2017	Baa2/A–/A	113.760	0.077	2.415
BANK AMER CORP	2.000%	Jan 2018	Baa2/A–/A	98.179	0.151	2.437
KROGER CO	3.850%	Aug 2023	Baa2/BBB/ BBB	99.384	0.367	3.924
PETROLEOS MEXICANOS	5.500%	Jan 2021	Baa1/BBB+	108.550	0.050	4.152
PETROBRAS GLOBAL FIN B V	4.375%	May 2023	A3//BBB	89.570	–1.369	5.786
AB SVENSK EXPORT KREDIT - SWEDISH EXPT CR	3.250%	Sept 2014	Aa1//	103.224	–0.045	0.297

In this report of actively traded bonds, the current yield on the Petrobras Global Fin B V bond that matures in May 2023 is 5.786%, or more than a full percentage point greater than the coupon rate of 4.375%. But the bond is trading at a discount, or less than par, at 89.570, or $895.70.

In contrast, the bond issued by Bank America Corporation with a coupon of 6% has a current yield of 2.415%, or more than three and a half percentage points less. That's because the last trading price was 113.760, or $1137.60, a substantial premium, or above par.

BUYING T-BILLS

New US Treasury bills are sold weekly through an auction process. Institutional investors, such as pension funds, submit written bids indicating the rate they are willing to pay and how many bills they want. One fund might offer 0.38%, for example, and another, 0.40%. Individual investors can submit noncompetitive bids through TreasuryDirect for the same auction, and have the purchase price debited directly from the checking account linked to their TreasuryDirect account.

The government fills the competitive orders at the lowest rate at which it can sell out the issue, and then fills all noncompetitive orders at the rate. For example, if the cut-off rate is 0.40%, all bidders at that rate and lower get bills.

When the bills mature, **par value** is deposited to your linked bank account or rolled over into new bills of the same term. The difference between the price you paid and the amount refunded or reinvested is the interest you earned.

BUYING TREASURY BONDS

US Treasury notes and bonds are the primary source of government borrowing. They're sold regularly at auction in $100 increments. You can buy just one or $5 million worth at one time through TreasuryDirect or your broker. The auction schedule is announced in advance on the website of the Bureau of the Fiscal Service (www.fiscal.treasury.gov).

All notes and bonds pay a fixed rate of interest that is set at auction. And you receive the total annual payment in two equal installments. At maturity you get par value back, whether you paid more or less than $100 to purchase them.

You can sell your notes and bonds before maturity by transferring them to your broker, dealer, or bank.

The price you receive for selling may be higher or lower than the price you paid to buy. To learn more, you can visit www.TreasuryDirect.gov.

Special Types of Bonds

There's something for everybody in the bond market. The challenge is finding the best choices for you.

You can choose different types of bonds to meet your financial needs, whether you're investing for college, looking for tax-free income, or want to limit risk to principal. That's why it's important to have a sense of the variety that's available, the special features they offer, and what their potential advantages and drawbacks are.

ZERO-COUPON BONDS

Zero-coupon bonds can be attractive investments because they're sold at a deep discount to par value, making them more affordable than other corporate or municipal issues. But there's a message in the name. *Coupon*, in bond terminology, means interest and, as the zero indicates, you receive no interest income during a zero's term. Instead, the interest is paid in a lump sum at maturity along with your purchase price. The accrued interest plus the issue price equals par value.

ZERO-COUPONS HAVE SOME DRAWBACKS

1. You must pay taxes on the interest that **accrues**, or is credited, each year even though you don't receive it. This doesn't apply if your zero-coupons are in a tax-deferred retirement account or you buy tax-exempt municipal zero-coupons.
2. The prices are extremely volatile in the secondary market, so you may lose money if you don't hold them to maturity.

One approach to using zeros is to buy them to mature when you need cash infusions: one for each year a tuition payment will be due, for example.

ASSET-BACKED SECURITIES

Asset-backed securities are fixed-income investments, as individual bonds are. But instead of being the debt of a single corporate or government issuer, an asset-backed security is constructed by combining debts of individual borrowers into a package, a process known as **securitization**, and selling slices of the package to investors.

Asset-backed securities may bundle automobile, credit card, education, or mortgage loans. Mortgage-backed securities (MBS) are the most common, and the best-known and least controversial MBS are Ginnie Maes, issued by the Government National Mortgage Association (GMNA), a corporation that's part of the federal government.

As the borrowers repay their loans, typically every month, those amounts—a combination of principal and interest that's characteristic of loan repayment—are passed through to the bondholders. That's different from income from individual bonds, which pay interest twice a year and repay principal at maturity.

Asset-backed securities tend to provide a slightly higher yield than bonds with similar ratings and terms. But because they are more complex than single securities, it can be more difficult to assess **credit risk**, which is the risk of default.

These investments may also be vulnerable to **interest rate risk**. If interest rates go up, loans made before the increase pay a lower rate than what's currently available. That means the market price of a MBS or other asset-backed security would drop. If the opposite occurs and rates drop, investors may confront **prepayment risk**, which means borrowers pay off their loans early, reducing investors' interest income.

A more complex type of asset-backed security, called a **collateralized debt obligation (CDO)**, is constructed from a pool of MBS. A CDO is rarely appropriate for, or marketed to, individual investors.

CALLABLE BONDS

Some bonds are issued with a **call provision**, which means the issuer has the right to repay principal before maturity and avoid repaying the interest that would have been due during the remainder of the term. Information about the first date on which a bond can be called is included in the offering.

Issuers will sometimes call bonds when interest rates drop, so they can reduce the cost of their debt. Investors, however, can lose expected income if their bonds are called, since they may have to reinvest their money at a lower rate.

Investors generally prefer bonds without call provisions. However, sometimes to make their callable bonds more attractive, issuers offer to pay a **premium**, or amount above par, if they exercise their right to call. The only drawback is that if the premium price is higher than the price you paid to buy, you may end up with a potentially taxable capital gain.

CONVERTIBLE BONDS

Convertible bonds offer you the option of acquiring stock instead of getting your principal back at maturity. The terms of the exchange—generally a certain number of shares for each $1,000 bond and when the conversion can be made—are spelled out in the initial offering.

Convertibles appeal to investors who think a corporation is growing and that the price of its stock is going up. The question is whether the potential for buying stock is worth the lower interest.

The initial interest rate is lower than the rate on other bonds with similar ratings being issued at the same time. But they typically provide higher yields than common stock while offering an opportunity to benefit from growth in the stock's value.

If the stock's price falls, and you choose not to exercise your right to convert, the bond is still likely to have value. That's more protection than if you'd bought the stock outright.

Two potential limitations are:

- Convertible bonds are among the least protected if the issuer defaults, so that you're unlikely to recover principal
- Many convertibles have call provisions, so if the price of the stock begins to rise, the issuer might recall the issue before you could convert

INSURED BONDS

Some municipal bonds have their principal and interest payments guaranteed by an insurance company. In exchange for that security, the bonds pay a lower rate of interest and the insurance company collects a fee from the issuer. One catch: If the insurer has financial problems, it could jeopardize the payments you expected.

BOND FUNDS

You can buy bond mutual funds rather than individual bonds. Most funds invest in specific types—like intermediate-term municipals, long-term corporates, or bonds of a particular state.

Perhaps the major advantage of using bond funds is that you can build a diversified bond portfolio at a more reasonable cost than you could if you were buying individual bonds.

But investing in bond funds isn't the same thing as buying a bond. When you buy a bond fund, you're buying shares of the fund, not the bonds that the fund owns. And bond fund managers don't usually buy and hold bonds until they mature. Rather, they trade them, sometimes frequently, in an effort to provide both yield and capital gains. When interest rates move higher, the value of the bonds the fund holds can drop and trades can produce capital losses. So the price you get when you redeem your shares may be more or less than you paid.

Investing in Mutual Funds

A mutual fund sells shares to raise the money it uses to invest in a portfolio of securities.

When you invest in a mutual fund, your money is pooled with that of other investors and used to make investments that are appropriate for the objective the specific fund is designed to achieve.

For example, a stock fund may buy stock in small companies to provide long-term growth in value. Or a bond fund might buy intermediate-term bonds to provide current income. The securities a fund holds are known as its **underlying investments**, and they make up the fund's **portfolio**.

In an **actively managed fund**, a professional manager chooses the stocks or bonds based on recommendations from the fund's team of research analysts. If it's an **index fund**, the fund invests in the stocks or bonds included in the particular index the fund tracks, such as the Standard & Poor's 500 stock index (S&P 500) or a Barclays Capital corporate bond index.

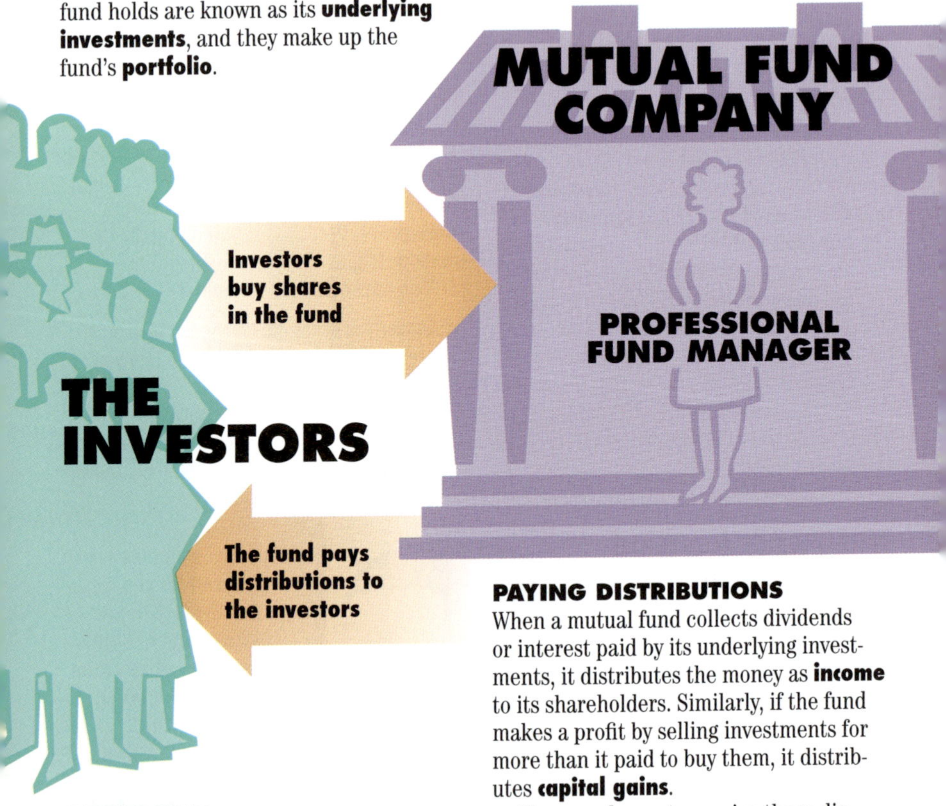

MUTUAL FUND COMPANY

Investors buy shares in the fund

PROFESSIONAL FUND MANAGER

THE INVESTORS

The fund pays distributions to the investors

PAYING DISTRIBUTIONS

When a mutual fund collects dividends or interest paid by its underlying investments, it distributes the money as **income** to its shareholders. Similarly, if the fund makes a profit by selling investments for more than it paid to buy them, it distributes **capital gains**.

You can choose to receive these distributions in cash or reinvest them to buy additional shares in the fund. Either way, the payments are taxable in the year they're paid unless you own the fund in a tax-deferred or tax-free account. In that case, reinvestment is automatic and no tax is due until you withdraw.

All funds are equity investments, including funds that invest in bonds. But your fund distributions are taxed based on the original source of the income. So income from interest is taxed at the same rate as your ordinary income, while income from qualifying dividends paid by most US corporations is taxed at the same rate as your long-term capital gains.

OPEN-END vs. CLOSED-END FUNDS

In an **open-end fund**, the more shares you—and other investors—want to buy, the more shares the fund sells. If you want to sell your shares, the fund buys them back at their current **net asset value (NAV)**.

Closed-end funds are traded on the major exchanges. There is a fixed number of shares available because the fund raises its money all at once. Shares may trade at a discount from or premium to their net asset value (NAV), depending on demand. Most funds that invest in a single country—like a Mexico fund—are closed-end.

LONG-TERM INVESTMENTS

Mutual funds are better suited to meet your expectations if you treat them as long-term investments. For example, those that emphasize growth may change very little in value in the short term, but may produce substantial returns over an extended period. The same is true for funds that emphasize value, or inexpensive securities that have the potential to be worth more in the future. And frequent buying and selling increases your trading costs and can reduce return.

That doesn't mean you should stick with a fund if its returns lag behind those of its peers over several years or if your investment goals change. But you should probably plan to hold funds if their disappointing results reflect what's happening in the market as a whole or in the segment of which they're a part. As the market cycle evolves, you'll be in a position to benefit if you still own shares as their value rises. The risk, of course, is that the fund's value may not rebound with the market.

WHAT TO LOOK FOR

- **Performance**
  How much the fund returns, whether the returns are consistent, and how they stack up against the returns of comparable funds. Be wary of any fund whose reputation is based on one or two stellar years and eight or nine dull ones.
- **Risk**
  How likely you are to earn money or lose it. Risk isn't bad if you're investing for the long term and you can tolerate some setbacks without selling in panic if the fund drops in value.
- **Costs**
  If you pay high commissions or fees, less of the money you put into your account is actually producing investment income. For example, if you pay a 5% commission on each $1,000 you put in, only $950 of it is actually invested.

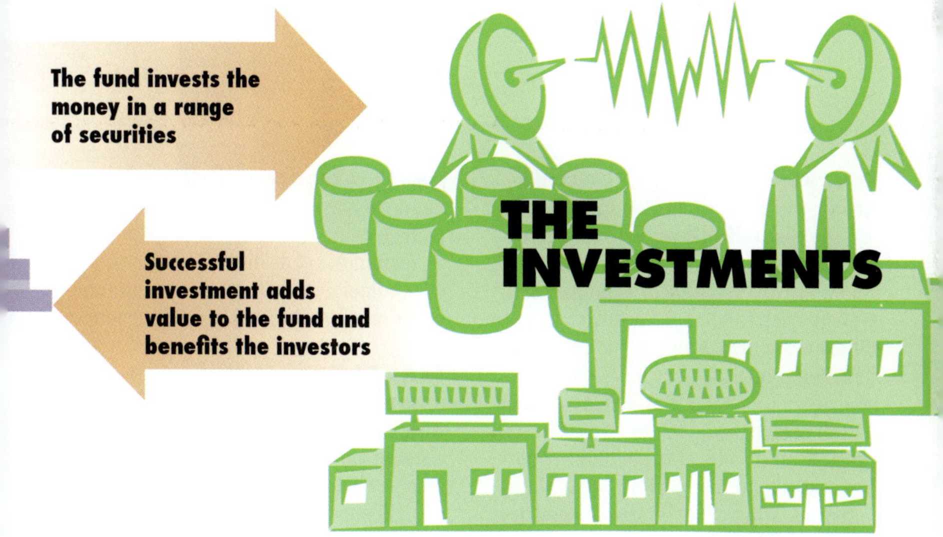

The fund invests the money in a range of securities

THE INVESTMENTS

Successful investment adds value to the fund and benefits the investors

LOAD vs. NO-LOAD FUNDS

If you buy a mutual fund through a broker, it will probably be a **load** fund, which means you pay a commission, typically between 2% and 5%. With a **front-end load** you pay when you make a purchase and sometimes on your dividend reinvestments as well. With a **back-end load** you pay when you redeem, or sell, your shares. With **level-load** funds, you pay a percentage of assets each year.

No-load funds, which you buy directly from the mutual fund company, have no commissions, but some funds may charge fees to cover sales and marketing costs.

DOLLAR COST AVERAGING

Dollar cost averaging means investing a fixed amount on a regular schedule, no matter what's happening in the financial markets. That way, the price you pay evens out over time, and you never pay only the highest or lowest price.

For example, if the price per share varies over a year from $10.65 to $8.45, you will have bought some high and some low. In the long run you may come out better than by trying to pinpoint the moment the price hits bottom or tops out. Dollar cost averaging doesn't mean, though, that you can't lose money, or that you can't realize a better return if you invest at the beginning of a market rise.

It's a Fund-Filled World

If you're looking for simplicity and variety, mutual funds may be the solution you're seeking.

Mutual funds simplify what many investors, maybe you included, find most intimidating: Figuring out what to buy and when to sell to meet particular goals or objectives. Because each fund is designed to meet a specific goal, your decisions are limited to choosing the funds you'll invest in and tracking how well they're doing in meeting your expectations.

FAMILIES OF FUNDS

Most mutual fund companies offer several different funds, known as a family, and let you move money back and forth among them. Individual funds within a family have different investment goals and strategies, reflecting the different interests of investors. One caution: Profit or loss from exchanges among funds must be reported to the IRS just as if you redeemed or sold the shares outright. Many investors own funds in several different families, choosing those with the best performance records or with the investment goals best suited to their needs.

DIVERSIFIED OPPORTUNITIES

Among the attractions of mutual funds are the **diversification** they can add to an investment portfolio. The funds themselves are diversified. For example, a typical stock fund might own 100 or more different securities within the category in which it invests—say large-company stocks, small-company stocks, or a combination of stocks and bonds in a **balanced fund**. Even if some of these underlying investments are not performing to their potential, others may be strong enough to offset that weakness and provide a positive return for the fund.

In addition, because there are so many types of funds available, each with its own **objective** and **investment style**, you can combine a number of different funds to create a diversified portfolio of equity and debt.

A fund's investment style describes the approach it takes to choosing investments. For example, following a **core** or **blend style**, a fund would buy both growth investments and value investments to take advantage of two approaches that tend to be successful at different times though infrequently at the same time. The logic is that the fund is ready for whatever is happening in the investment markets. A **contrarian style**, on the other hand, means buying securities that other managers are avoiding.

As important as diversification is, however, remember that it doesn't guarantee a profit or prevent losses in a falling market.

TARGET DATE FUNDS

A **target date fund** is a fund of funds with a very specific objective: to build account value that will ultimately generate income that helps to provide a more financially secure retirement. It's constructed from a number of different funds, usually from the same family, and over time the emphasis is shifted from a focus on stock funds—which are equated with growth—to a focus on bond funds—which are equated with income.

The fund companies that sponsor target date funds offer several funds simultaneously, each with a different end point, or target date. They're typically spaced in five- or ten-year intervals: 2015, 2020, 2025, 2030, and so on. You select the one with the date closest to the date you plan to retire.

Among the things to consider with a target date fund in addition to its fees and past performance are the allocation that the fund aims for at its target date,

FILLING A NEED

One reason mutual funds appeal to many people is that funds offer a way to diversify relatively easily. And, because the funds do the research, make the buy and sell decisions, handle the paperwork, and provide regular updates on performance, funds take some of the complexity out of investing.

Equally important, the relatively small amounts of money required to open and add to an account mean that you can put your money to work more quickly though your return is not guaranteed.

Impact investing attracts investors committed to addressing pressing social and environmental issues while realizing a positive return.

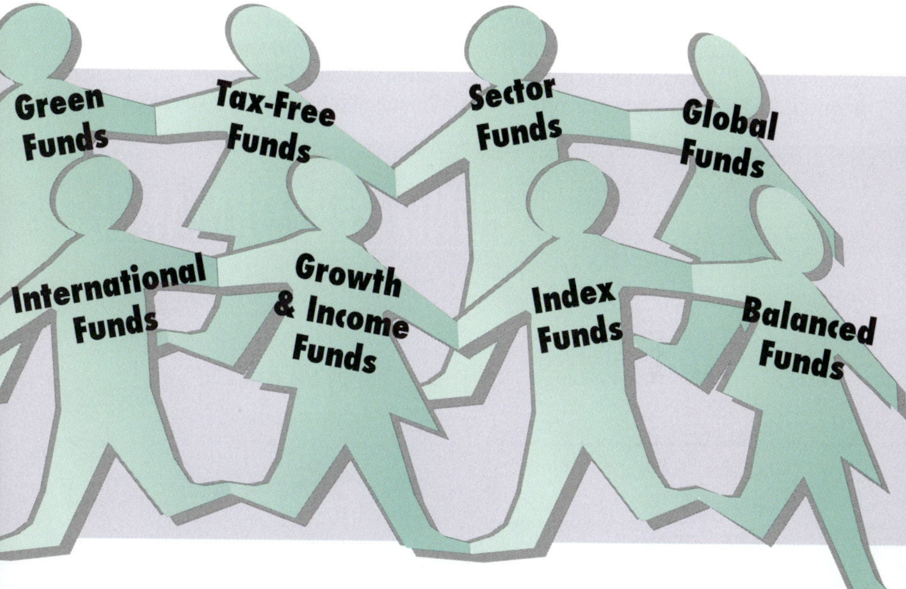

whether the allocation will continue to change, when it will reach its most conservative point, and when the fund expects investors to start to withdraw.

EXCHANGE TRADED FUNDS

Exchange traded funds (ETFs) resemble mutual funds in some ways and individual stocks in others. With an ETF, you buy and sell shares in the collective performance of a portfolio of stocks or bonds included in an index—similar to trading shares in an index fund. Each ETF has a **net asset value (NAV)** calculated the same way that a mutual fund's NAV is calculated.

But you trade ETFs as you do stocks, as prices change throughout the day. And you can use traditional stock trading techniques, including stop and limit orders, margin purchases, and short sales.

One major advantage is that ETFs don't have to sell shares to accommodate shareholder redemptions, minimizing portfolio turnover and the potential tax consequences of resulting capital gains. And they tend to have lower expense ratios than most mutual funds.

On the other hand, you may pay a brokerage commission each time you trade an ETF unless you buy through a brokerage firm that waives commissions on at least some ETFs.

INVESTING OVERSEAS

Mutual funds and exchange traded funds (ETFs) are convenient and often cost-effective ways to diversify your portfolio by investing in international markets. You can find a range of stock and bond funds, from the broadly based to the narrowly focused, offered by a number of fund companies. The mutual funds may be either actively managed or index funds, while nearly all ETFs are index funds.

The advantages of investing abroad include the opportunity to benefit from economic growth in various parts of the world as well as providing a hedge against disappointing results at home. And using funds to expand your portfolio means that tax and other issues are handled for you. But you do have to be aware of the risks that fluctuating currency values and political unrest pose to your return.

Socially responsible funds attract investors with strong political or social commitments who want to invest in companies whose policies they agree with.

Anatomy of a Prospectus

By law, mutual funds must provide detailed information before they accept your money. Dissecting a fund's prospectus reveals its inner workings.

Mutual fund companies provide a **prospectus** for each fund they offer. It includes a statement of objectives, a description of how the fund operates, a summary of its investments, risks, expense ratio, and information about its management.

Annual and **quarterly reports** give details about past performance as well as the fund's investments. Companies will also supply a **Statement of Additional Information (SAI)**, which has detailed financial information, if you ask for it.

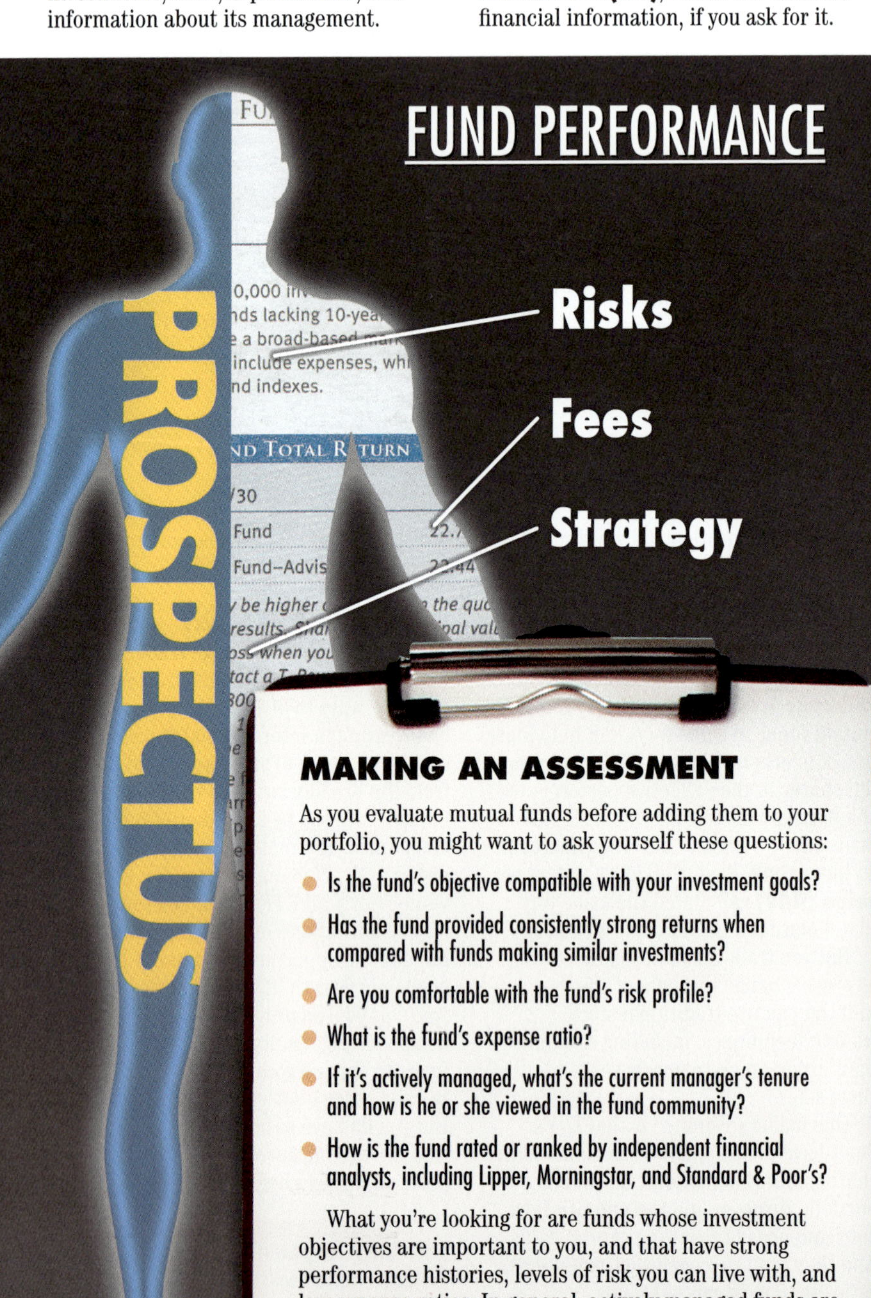

MAKING AN ASSESSMENT

As you evaluate mutual funds before adding them to your portfolio, you might want to ask yourself these questions:

- Is the fund's objective compatible with your investment goals?
- Has the fund provided consistently strong returns when compared with funds making similar investments?
- Are you comfortable with the fund's risk profile?
- What is the fund's expense ratio?
- If it's actively managed, what's the current manager's tenure and how is he or she viewed in the fund community?
- How is the fund rated or ranked by independent financial analysts, including Lipper, Morningstar, and Standard & Poor's?

What you're looking for are funds whose investment objectives are important to you, and that have strong performance histories, levels of risk you can live with, and low expense ratios. In general, actively managed funds are more expensive than index funds, and international funds are more expensive that domestic ones.

FEES AFFECT YOUR RETURN

When you invest in mutual funds, you pay a number of fees that don't apply when you own individual securities. While you may be able to avoid some fees, including redemption fees for selling within a restricted period, you can't avoid asset-based operating expenses that all shareholders pay. They're calculated daily and subtracted from the fund's net assets before investment gains or losses are credited to your account. The higher the fees, the more earnings potential you sacrifice.

Operating expenses, which include management fees and administrative fees, are quoted as an expense ratio, or percentage of a fund's net assets. Ratios vary from company to company, and from one fund to another within the same fund. Trading costs, which also affect return, are not included in the expense ratio.

A PRIMARY SOURCE

A mutual fund must provide a prospectus when you buy shares in the fund, but it's smarter to request a copy or read it online before you buy. If the fund offers a Summary Prospectus, it will provide what you need in a more accessible format.

Take a look at the section describing the fund's **objectives** and the **strategies** it uses to achieve them. Funds that seem similar can produce very different results based on the investment approach the manager uses and what's happening in the economy as a whole. For example, a small cap growth fund is likely to have a stronger return than a small growth value fund in some periods and a weaker return in others. This section also explains which, if any, derivative investments the fund uses and how it invests to offset risk.

All mutual funds expose you to investment **risk** that can have a major impact on return. In discussing risks, a prospectus focuses on those that have particular relevance for the fund, such as interest rate risk for a long-term bond fund or exchange rate risk for an international fund.

In discussing fund performance over the past ten years, or as long as it has existed if it's less than ten, the prospectus identifies the **benchmark** or benchmarks against which it measures its performance. It's typically a major market index. Of course, past performance doesn't guarantee future results, but it does illustrate how the fund has fared in market ups and downs.

WHAT A SHARE COSTS

The dollar value of one share of a fund's stock is its **net asset value (NAV)**. It's figured by adding up the value of all the fund's holdings, subtracting expenses, and dividing by the number of outstanding shares. If you buy a no-load fund, you pay the NAV when you buy shares.

Front-load funds charge you more than the NAV to buy because commissions are figured in, but they may pay you straight net asset value when you sell.

$$\frac{\text{Fund holdings} - \text{Expenses}}{\text{\# of Outstanding Shares}} = \text{NAV}$$

FUND PERFORMANCE

You can evaluate fund performance by looking at three factors:

- **Change in NAV**
- **Total return**
- **Yield**

An increase in NAV is a positive sign because it means the value of the underlying investments has increased, while a decrease in NAV means a loss in value. But because NAV is also affected by the number of outstanding shares and fund expenses, it's not necessarily the most reliable performance indicator.

A fund's **total return** is the percentage it has increased or decreased in value, including reinvested distributions. Funds report this figure for various time periods, though these results may not be identical to your actual return based on the date you invested and other factors. For periods longer than one year, return is annualized and reflects composite gains and losses over the period.

Fund **yield** is the amount of income a fund provides as a percentage of its NAV.

With that information, you can compare similar funds to each other or evaluate a fund's total return and yield in relation to the other ways you could have invested your principal. In making comparisons, you can use a market index that's appropriate for the type of investments the fund makes, such as the S&P 500 for large company funds, or an appropriate mutual fund index.

Options and Futures

To add some variety to your portfolio, you might consider options and futures.

Options and futures contracts are **derivative investments**. That means their price at any given time depends on the changing value of the underlying product, also called an instrument. You can buy options on stocks, stock and bond indexes, interest rates, currency values, and futures contracts. You can buy futures contracts on agricultural or financial products, natural resources, interest rates, and currency values. And you can buy either to **hedge** or to **speculate**.

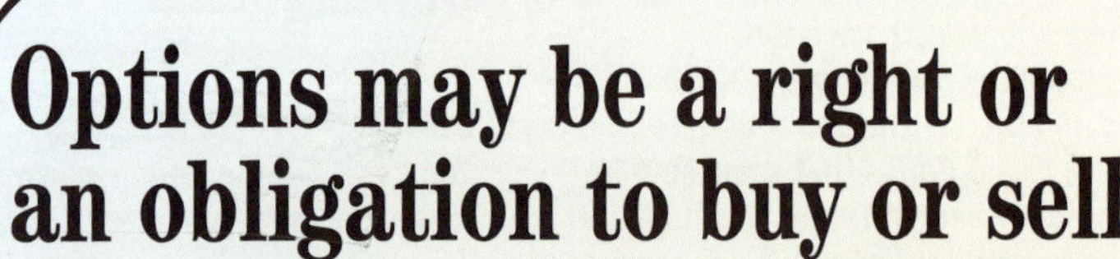

Options may be a right or an obligation to buy or sell

If you buy options, you may choose to buy or sell. If you sell options, you may have to buy or sell.

Buying an option gives you the right to decide whether or not you want to buy or sell an underlying instrument, such as shares of a stock, a futures contract, or various financial products, at an agreed-upon price, called the **strike price**, before a specific **expiration date**. You lose only the **premium**, or the price of the option, if you don't **exercise**, or act on, the option. But you may be able to buy at a good price, hedge potential losses, or offset your cost.

Selling an option means you must go through with a trade if an investor who bought the option decides to exercise it. The most common, and least risky, options for individual investors to sell are **covered stock options**, which means you own the underlying stock and have it available to sell. In addition, you collect a premium when you sell the options.

CONVERTING TRADES

Options can be sold for a profit before the expiration date or neutralized with an offsetting order. Unlike most futures contracts, though, options tend to be exercised when the underlying item reaches the strike price. That's because part of the appeal of call options — stock calls in particular — is that they can be converted to actual investments, often at an attractive price.

WHAT KINDS OF OPTIONS ARE THERE?

All options fall into two broad categories: **puts** and **calls**. You can buy or sell either.

	Calls	**Puts**
BUY *(go long)*	The right to buy the underlying instrument at a fixed price until the expiration date	The right to sell the underlying instrument at a fixed price until the expiration date
SELL *(go short)*	The obligation to sell the underlying instrument if the option holder exercises the option (known as writing a call)	The obligation to buy the underlying instrument if the option holder exercises the option (known as writing a put)

WHAT OPTIONS COST

The premium, or nonrefundable price of an option, depends on a number of factors:

- The type of underlying instrument the option is on
- The difference between the underlying instrument's price and the strike price, or what it would cost to exercise the option
- The current state of the financial markets and what's expected to happen
- The time remaining until expiration

If you buy options, you start out with a **debit**. That means you've spent money you can recover only if you sell your option or exercise it. In those cases, you subtract the cost of the premium from any income you realize to find your net profit.

As a seller, on the other hand, you begin with a **credit** because you collect the premium. If the option is never exercised, you keep the money.

Futures are obligations to buy or sell

A futures contract is a deal you make now to buy or sell a commodity in the future.

When you buy or sell a futures contract, you're making a deal now to buy or sell a product in the future. But product prices, and therefore contract prices, can change dramatically during the life of the contract as a result of changes in supply and demand as well as other market pressures.

The futures market benefits **hedgers**, who produce or use commodities or who own large investment portfolios, because they want to avoid risk by locking in a price. For example, a baking company might buy a futures contract to buy wheat at a set price so that a potential crop failure won't increase its production costs.

Speculators, on the other hand, aren't interested in the commodity, but buy and sell futures contracts because they're willing to take risks that prices will rise or fall in the direction they predict. They can make — or lose — large amounts of money because they **leverage** their purchase, which means investing a small amount — often 10% — to purchase a futures contract worth much more. For example, a speculator might buy a wheat contract worth $17,500 for $1,750.

OFFSETTING CONTRACTS

While some futures contracts result in commodities changing hands, most contracts are **offset** when the investor buys an opposing contract. That is, someone with a contract to buy offsets it by buying a contract to sell the same product.

One of the reasons that futures trading can be so hectic is that profit or loss can depend on very small price differences, which must be acted on quickly. And if prices drop sharply, it can be difficult to act quickly enough to prevent big losses.

WHERE YOU TRADE

You can trade futures contracts on commodities exchanges, futures and options exchanges, certain stock markets, and over the counter. While some individual investors participate in the market, they're often more likely to get involved by investing in **managed futures accounts**. Most futures transactions, especially trading in financial futures like currency values and interest rates, are carried out by institutional investors, such as pension funds or mutual funds.

Investing in Real Estate

You may buy property to stake a claim, but real estate is also a good way to diversify your portfolio.

Investing in real estate can range from owning your home to being a partner in a major construction project, and from buying a cabin in the woods to owning a castle in Spain.

If you borrow, or use **leverage**, to pay for your investment, selling at a profit can mean a healthy return. But leverage also magnifies your losses if prices go down.

A primary appeal of real estate investing has been that prices have sometimes increased substantially, though a primary drawback is that it's sometimes hard to sell, especially at the price you want, when the real estate market is weak.

VACATION AND RETIREMENT PROPERTY

Second homes appeal to investors who buy them either as an investment or primarily for their own use but welcome the extra income that renting can provide. Complex rules limit their usefulness as tax shelters, and overbuilding has cut resale value in some areas.

Real Estate Investing

THE PLUSES

- Provides a hedge against inflation
- Permits tax deductions in some cases
- Produces sizeable profits in some markets in some periods

AND THE MINUSES

- May be difficult to sell quickly
- May be overpriced in some markets and undervalued in others
- Subject to zoning laws, environmental issues

REAL ESTATE INVESTMENT TRUSTS

REIT

REITs are funds that trade like stocks and resemble mutual funds. Your investment is pooled with other people's, and the REIT invests it.

For many people REITs are attractive real estate investments because the trust makes the investment decisions, it's easy to trade the shares, and the yields can be high. REIT share prices fluctuate in response to market conditions, the distributions the trust pays, and changes in real estate values. Long-term profitability depends on the underlying value of the properties and the quality of the management.

Equity REITs buy properties that produce income or have growth potential. Some buy only certain types of property, while others diversify. In general, well-established equity REITs have been better investments than **mortgage** REITs, which invest in real estate loans, start-up offerings, or hybrid REITs that combine equity and mortgage investments.

MORE THAN JUST RETURN

It can be harder to figure the return on a real estate investment — especially if the property is also your home — than on other investments you make. Part of your investment cost pays for a place for you to live. You get tax breaks on your mortgage interest and your local taxes. And you won't owe capital gains tax on up to $500,000 profit when you sell ($250,000 if you're single), if you meet the requirements to qualify.

EMPTY LAND

Called unimproved or raw property, empty land is usually the most speculative and the least liquid real estate investment. If you pay high taxes or have big carrying costs, it's hard to make money.

RENTAL PROPERTY

Rentals are traditional real estate investments. The key to making money is to charge at least enough to cover the mortgage, insurance, taxes, and repairs.

Among the advantages of rental property:

- You can deduct all your repair and improvement expenses up to the amount of rent you collect. You may also be able to deduct losses on your investment against your regular income
- Buying rental property to fix up and sell can produce a big profit if the market is right, but frustrations and big losses if it's not

But there are also potential disadvantages:

- If rents drop or space stays empty, you could end up losing money instead of profiting from your investment
- Owning rental property makes you a landlord, which is an investment of time and energy

LIMITED PARTNERSHIPS

Limited partnerships invest in income-producing properties, often of a particular type like shopping malls or low-income housing, or in a specific geographic area.

The appeal is that several **limited partners** pooling their money can invest in larger properties with the potential for greater profits. The limited partners have no management responsibility and no liability beyond their investment.

Nontraded limited partnerships, including nontraded REITs, are restricted to high-net worth investors and established for a set period of time, often seven to twelve years. Most have large fees, are difficult—maybe impossible—to get out of, and provide no assurance of return on investment. But they may provide large distributions, plus portfolio diversification because their returns aren't linked to equity markets.

Paying Taxes

Taxes pay the bills of the government that collects them.

The basic structure of US tax law—a progressive tax system under which those with larger incomes pay tax at a higher rate than those with smaller incomes—has been in place since the 16th amendment to the US Constitution was adopted in 1913. But tax provisions change all the time, as Congress passes new laws that expand or amend the **Internal Revenue Code (IRC)**, sets new tax rates, and authorizes the way that tax revenue is spent.

The **Internal Revenue Service (IRS)**, which is part of the US Department of the Treasury, interprets the revenue code through a series of regulations, collects the taxes that are due—primarily through payroll withholding—and provides the forms and instructions that you use to file your return.

Federal income taxes aren't the only money that's withheld from your pay. So are state and local income taxes, and Social Security and Medicare taxes, as required by the **Federal Insurance Contribution Act (FICA)**. Union dues, if you owe them, are also withheld. And you can choose to have contributions to employer sponsored retirement savings plans, premiums for health insurance, and amounts for other benefits or obligations withheld from your paycheck as well.

You receive a copy of **IRS Form W-2** from your employer every January that reports your income, including any extra benefits you received and the amounts that were withheld. You file copies of the W-2 with your federal and state tax returns and keep one for your records.

HELP FROM THE IRS

The IRS website, www.irs.gov, is a valuable resource for

HIGHLIGHTS IN THE HISTORY OF INCOME TAX

1862

The first income taxes were imposed by the US government to pay for the Civil War. Collected between 1863 and 1871, they were very unpopular and were repealed in 1872.

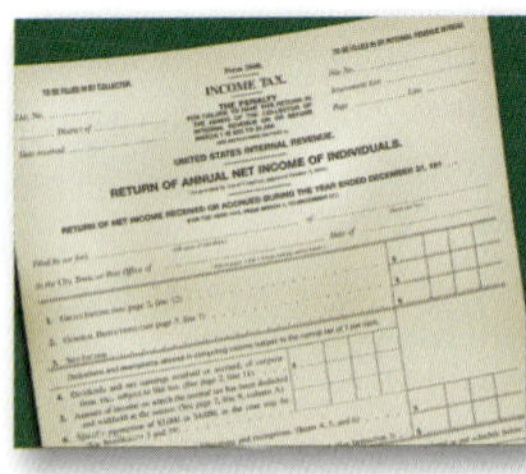

1909

A constitutional amendment was proposed to permit a personal income tax. It was ratified by the required 36 states in 1913 and became law. Taxes have been collected ever since.

1943

Withholding was introduced in 1943 to provide a steady stream of income to fund the costs of waging World War II.

GIVE AND TAKE
In most cases you can deduct the cost of tax preparation, including software programs, tax publications you purchase, and electronic filing fees. You take the deduction for the tax year you actually incur the cost, which is typically the year following the one for which the return is due.

answers to many of the questions you may have about federal income taxes. Among other things, you can download publications and forms, use the interactive tax assistance link, and e-file your return. You can also call the IRS to order forms and publications, ask questions, and find help resolving filing and tax issues.

The Volunteer Income Tax Assistance (VITA) program provides IRS-certified volunteers to work with taxpayers who need help preparing and filing their returns, including the elderly, disabled, and those with limited English skills. One of the program's main goals is to make sure that these taxpayers know about the credits and deductions they're entitled to claim. There's also a separate Tax Counseling for the Elderly (TCE) program.

You can check Publication 910, *"IRS Guide to Free Tax Services,"* for more information.

PROFESSIONAL HELP

Professional tax preparers charge a fee to prepare your return and help you reduce your tax bill by capitalizing on relevant provisions of the IRC. **Registered tax return preparers** are required to have a preparer tax identification number (PTIN) and pass a competency test and tax compliance check. There are also **enrolled agents**, who are accredited by the IRS and certified by the Treasury, and licensed or **certified public accountants (CPAs)** who are tax specialists. The more complex your tax situation, the more important it becomes to work with a preparer who has extensive experience with similar situations. You may also want to consult a tax attorney and coordinate a collaboration between your preparer and your financial adviser.

Before you choose a preparer, however, you should check the firm's or individual's credentials and get answers to questions such as:

- What training and certification do you have as a tax preparer?
- Will you be available to answer questions throughout the year?
- What help will you provide if I am audited?
- How much will preparing my return cost?

TIME TO E-FILE
According to the IRS, more than 122 million tax returns—about 83% of all returns—were e-filed in 2013. Professional tax return preparers with 11 or more clients must e-file their returns. Those taxpayers who don't use a preparer can either e-file for free on the IRS website or use tax preparation software to e-file.

1953
The agency's name was changed from Bureau of Internal Revenue to Internal Revenue Service.

1986
Congress passed a major overhaul of tax legislation, the Tax Reform Act, which had more than 300 provisions and took three years to implement. Limited electronic filing of tax returns began.

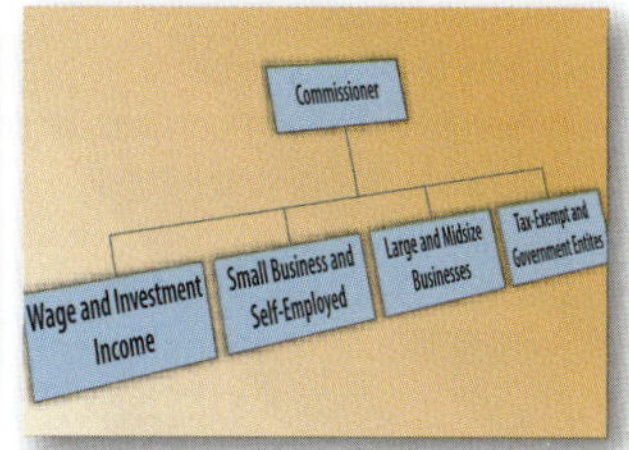

2000
The IRS made major structural changes, the biggest since 1953. It instituted four operating divisions: Wage and Investment, Small Business and Self-Employed, Large and Mid-Sized Business, and Tax-Exempt and Government Entities.

Completing a Return

When you're ready to file, you add up your income and figure out what, if anything, you owe.

You file your income tax return either electronically or on paper using the form that best suits your income and the deductions or credits you'll claim.

Each form comes with its own set of instructions, explaining line by line what to do. There are also a number of workcharts to help you make detailed calculations or resolve whether you're eligible for certain credits, deductions, or exemptions.

The instructions also refer you to IRS publications that provide more information, and to the supplemental forms that you may need to file as backup.

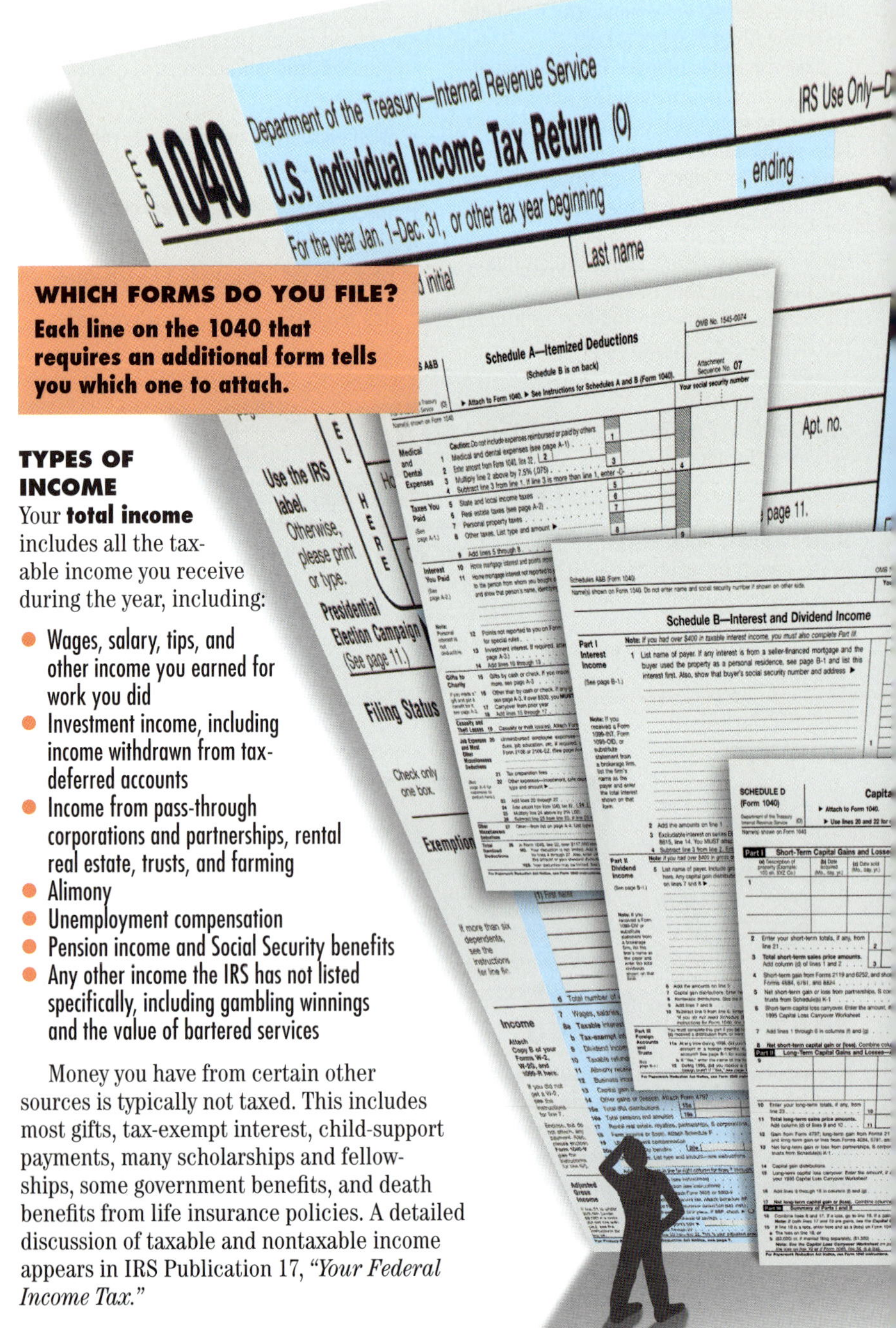

WHICH FORMS DO YOU FILE?

Each line on the 1040 that requires an additional form tells you which one to attach.

TYPES OF INCOME

Your **total income** includes all the taxable income you receive during the year, including:

- Wages, salary, tips, and other income you earned for work you did
- Investment income, including income withdrawn from tax-deferred accounts
- Income from pass-through corporations and partnerships, rental real estate, trusts, and farming
- Alimony
- Unemployment compensation
- Pension income and Social Security benefits
- Any other income the IRS has not listed specifically, including gambling winnings and the value of bartered services

Money you have from certain other sources is typically not taxed. This includes most gifts, tax-exempt interest, child-support payments, many scholarships and fellowships, some government benefits, and death benefits from life insurance policies. A detailed discussion of taxable and nontaxable income appears in IRS Publication 17, *"Your Federal Income Tax."*

FROM TOTAL INCOME TO TAX OWED

Total income
– Adjustments
= ADJUSTED GROSS INCOME

Adjusted gross income
– Exemptions and deductions
= TAXABLE INCOME

Income tax you owe
– Credits
+ Other taxes you owe
= TOTAL TAX

Total tax
– Withholding and estimated-tax payments
= REFUND OR PAYMENT DUE

When you barter, you exchange something you have for something you need, or you exchange a service you can perform for a service you need done. No money changes hands. But legally you must report the value of the goods or services you received as income.

Adjustments are amounts you can subtract from your total income for certain retirement, education, and self-employment expenses, alimony, and moving expenses.

Adjusted gross income (AGI) is your income minus adjustments. If your AGI is more than a certain amount set by Congress, you can't deduct your IRA contribution, and your adjustments, exemptions, and itemized deductions may be limited.

Exemptions reduce your income by letting you subtract a fixed amount of money for yourself, your spouse, and each of your dependents. Exemptions are reduced for some taxpayers based on AGI and are eliminated entirely for others.

Deductions are amounts you can subtract for certain personal expenses. Most taxpayers use the standard deduction, which is a fixed dollar amount set for each year. Or, you can **itemize**, or list, your deductions and subtract that amount subject to AGI limits.

Taxable income is the amount on which you owe tax. You look up the tax using the tax tables (for amounts up to $100,000) or figure what you owe using the tax rate schedules.

Credits are subtracted from the tax you owe. The childcare credit and credit for the elderly and disabled let you subtract money you paid other people to care for your dependents, up to a set limit.

Other taxes include amounts you may owe that aren't accounted for in the income section, such as taxes on household employment and self-employment.

Payments include amounts that were withheld and forwarded to the IRS, estimated tax payments, and certain credits not subtracted earlier.

Refund or **tax payment due** is determined by subtracting your payments from the total tax that's due. If you've paid more than you owe, you get a refund. If you haven't paid enough, you must pay the outstanding balance due.

Tax Status and Brackets

There's a two-step process for determining the rate at which you pay income tax.

The income tax you owe the federal government depends on two factors: your **filing status** and the highest of seven possible **tax brackets** into which a portion of your taxable income falls.

There are five categories of filing status:

- Single
- Married filing jointly
- Married filing separately
- Head of household
- Qualifying widow(er) with dependent child

You must follow IRS guidelines in selecting the one that most accurately reflects your situation as of December 31 of the tax year. Some options can save you money, such as filing as head of household instead of single, if you qualify. Others almost always cost more, such a filing separately rather than jointly if you're married.

Taxable income is divided into seven brackets with floors and ceilings set annually—though the top bracket has no ceiling—and generally adjusted upward each year to account for inflation. In fact, there are really three sets of seven brackets: one set for married filing jointly and qualifying widow(er)s, one for head of household, and one for single and married filing separately.

THE RATE YOU PAY

Each bracket is taxed at a different rate, with the lowest rate—10%—applying to the bottom bracket and the highest rate—39.6%—applying to the top bracket. The rates for the other brackets in 2014 are 15%, 25%, 28%,

SINGLE TAXPAYER WITH A TAXABLE INCOME OF $120,000

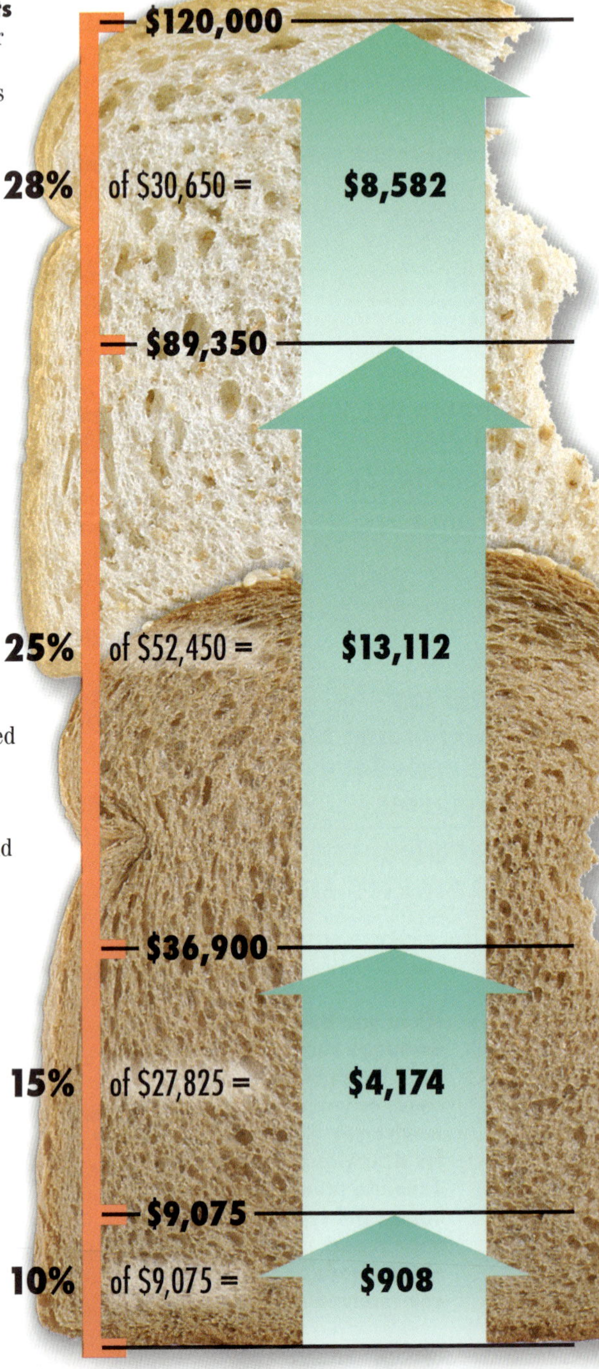

TOTAL TAX DUE = $26,776

Tax rates for 2014. Brackets cover different ranges of income in different tax years.

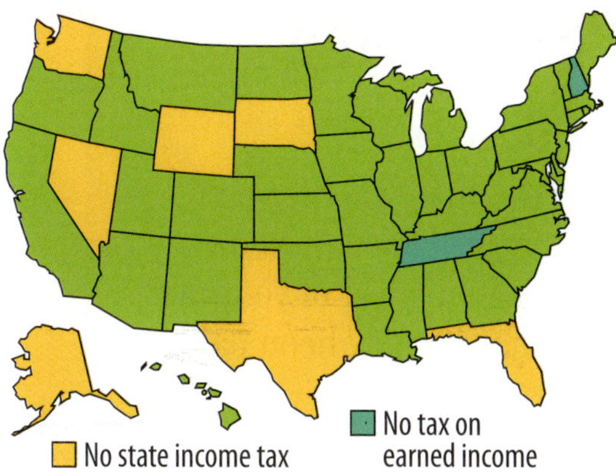

33%, and 35%. The portion of your income that falls into each bracket is taxed at the rate for that bracket.

For example, if the last dollar of your taxable income falls into the 28% bracket, you'd pay some tax at 10%, some at 15%, some at 25%, and some at 28%. The top rate at which you pay is called your **marginal rate**. That's in contrast to your **effective rate**, which you calculate by dividing your total tax by your taxable income. Your effective rate is always lower than your marginal rate.

DIFFERENT TAX BITES

As an example of how the system works, a hypothetical single taxpayer with a taxable income of $120,000 would pay $26,776 in taxes for tax year 2014, crossing four tax brackets. Her marginal rate is 28%, and her effective rate is 22%. A married couple filing a joint return with the same $120,000 of taxable income would owe $21,713 across three tax brackets. That's a marginal rate of 25% and an effective rate of 18%.

In contrast, if each person of a married couple earned $120,000, for a joint total of $240,000, they would owe $55,105, or $1,553 more than if each of them were single. Their marginal rate would be 33% and their effective rate 23%. But by filing separate returns as a married couple, they'd take an even bigger hit, owing $59,229. That marginal rate is 39.6% and the effective rate is 25%.

ALTERNATIVE MINIMUM TAX

The **alternative minimum tax (AMT)** is a parallel tax system that was created to ensure that high-income taxpayers couldn't avoid paying their fair share of taxes by capitalizing on tax loopholes. It hasn't actually worked that way, as many loopholes still exist. But what has happened is that the AMT increasingly affects middle-income taxpayers with perfectly legitimate but higher-than-average exemptions or deductible expenses. These include state and local taxes, mortgage interest, or rental income. To determine what you owe, you must figure your tax both ways and pay the higher amount.

STATE AND LOCAL TAXES

Everyone who earns income in the United States, and US citizens who earn income elsewhere in the world, must pay federal income taxes. You also pay state income taxes unless you reside in one of the seven states that don't collect them: Alaska, Florida, Nevada, South Dakota, Texas, Washington, and Wyoming. Two others—New Hampshire and Tennessee—tax interest and dividend income but not earned income.

The good news is that you can deduct any state and local income taxes you've paid when you file your federal tax return, provided you itemize your deductions. That helps to reduce your taxable income, though it may make you vulnerable to the AMT.

OTHER TYPES OF TAXES

All but five states—Alaska, Delaware, Montana, New Hampshire, and Oregon—and many local governments charge **sales tax** on the value of most or all of the goods and services you pay for. And most states or local governments levy **property taxes** on the value of real estate or personal property, or both. These taxes pay for public services, such as the public school system and police, fire, and sanitation services.

Federal and state governments also charge **excise taxes** on the manufacture, sale, or use of certain products, such as tobacco, petroleum products, alcohol, car rentals, and hotel rooms.

The federal government imposes **gift and estate taxes** on assets transferred from one owner to another if the total value of those assets reaches a certain limit. In 2014, it's $5,340,000. The exceptions are gifts to qualifying charitable organizations and to spouses who are US citizens. However, annual gifts of up to $14,000 to an individual are federally tax free. (Both those limits will be adjusted for inflation over time.) Some states also have estate or inheritance taxes.

Prepaying Taxes

By the time you file your tax return or request an extension, most of your tax bill has already been paid.

Most people prepay the income tax they owe through **payroll withholding**, quarterly **estimated payments**, or a combination of the two. This isn't because they want to, but because the IRS generally requires it. In fact, the IRS may impose a penalty if the balance due on your tax return exceeds the amount you prepaid by more than 10%, or, in some cases, more than $1,000.

What's more, if your AGI for the previous tax year was more than $150,000, you must prepay either 90% of your expected tax or 110% of what you owed in the previous tax year.

HOW WITHHOLDING WORKS

If you earn wages or a salary, taxes are generally withheld from each paycheck and from any bonuses and commissions. Taxes are also withheld on sick pay you receive from your employer as well as from unemployment compensation.

With some other types of income, the situation is more complicated. For example, the way your employer accounts for tips you receive or taxable fringe benefits, such as the personal use of an employer's car, may mean not enough is withheld. You must also decide whether to authorize withholding from any pensions, annuity payments, and Social Security.

There's a detailed discussion of withholding issues in Section 4 of IRS Publication 17. It pays to take a look.

DEALING WITH THE W-4

Your employer determines the amount to withhold from your earnings based on the information you provide on **IRS Form W-4**. You must complete this form whenever you begin a new job and should revise it any time your personal or tax situation changes.

In addition to your name and Social Security number, you indicate your marital status and choose the number of **allowances** you claim. While providing that information seems pretty straightforward, it's sometimes a challenge. One reason is that you're trying to come as close as you can to aligning the amount that's withheld with what you'll actually owe in taxes for the year. Having too much withheld means you're making an interest-free loan to the federal government. But having too little withheld means you risk a big tax bill and maybe a penalty.

Deciding on your allowances can be complicated if you work two or more jobs, if both you and your spouse work and file a joint return, if you pay self-employment tax, or if you have a high-income job or substantial investment

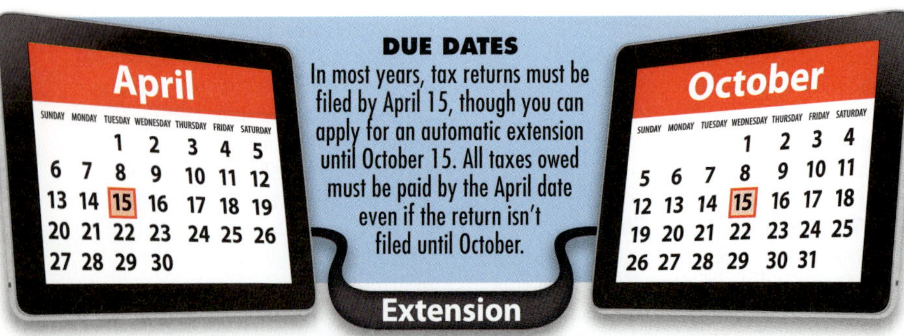

income. The IRS provides worksheets to help you come as close to the right amount as you can. It may help to have your previous year's tax return handy, especially your itemized deductions (Schedule A) and your interest and dividend income (Schedule B). You can also use the IRS Withholding Calculator at www.irs.gov/individuals/IRS-Withholding-Calculator.

ROLL THOSE DICE

If you have more than $5,000 in gambling winnings, or collect 300 times the amount you bet on any wager, 25% of your take must be withheld for taxes. And that rate goes up to 28% on winnings as small as $600 if you don't give the payer your Social Security number. But there is good news, of sorts. You can deduct gambling losses up to, but not more than, your winnings. You have to itemize your deductions and support your claims with a detailed accounting of your activities.

ESTIMATED TAXES

If your withholding doesn't cover the taxes you owe, or you have nothing withheld because you're self-employed, unemployed, or live on unearned income, you must pay estimated taxes four times a year, in April, June, September, and January using IRS Form 1040-ES.

The first payment is due for the first quarter in which you have taxable income. You can pay everything you expect to owe at that time or you can pay in installments. It's fairly easy if your income is predictable, but more difficult if it's not—as may be the case if you're self-employed.

You can recalculate the tax you owe each quarter to find what you must pay in each remaining installment. You may owe a penalty if you underpay a quarterly amount even if you end up with a refund when you file your return. It's probably smart to work with a tax adviser who specializes in this area.

UNUSUAL SITUATIONS

If you're expecting a substantial one-time payment in addition to your regular salary or wages—perhaps a retroactive payment as a result of a renegotiated contract or a back pay adjustment—you may want to redo your W-4 to temporarily increase the number of allowances. That way, you can potentially avoid having more withheld than the tax you'll owe. Once you receive the payment, you simply go back to the number of allowances that more accurately reflects your normal situation.

But you don't want to claim too many allowances as a general practice. If the IRS uncovers a chronic problem with withholding, it may issue what's known as a lock-in letter to your employer that specifies the maximum number of allowances you may claim. There is an appeals process if you don't agree.

FYI

The IRS publishes a detailed discussion of tax prepayment in Publication 505, *"Tax Withholding and Estimated Tax,"* which is updated each year.

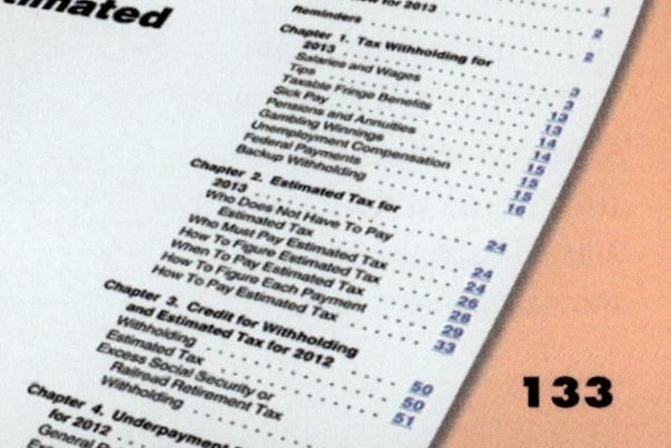
Publication 505

Tax Withholding and Estimated Tax

Contents

Tax Planning

You can legitimately reduce the tax you owe by planning ahead.

The most effective way to pay the least tax that you are legally obligated to pay is to make financial decisions with an eye to their tax consequences. For example, one way to reduce your current income tax is to contribute to a **tax-deferred retirement account**, such as an employer-sponsored plan. Your contribution reduces the income that's reported to the IRS and as a result, the current tax you owe. Any earnings in the account are also tax deferred.

Of course, when you take money out of the account after you retire, you'll owe tax on the full amount of your withdrawal. But you may be paying at a lower tax rate when you take money out than you were when you put it in. In some sense it's a gamble, but thanks to the power of compounding, it's possible to come out significantly ahead, even if tax rates have increased.

Or, if you aren't earning as much now as you expect to in the future, you might choose to put aside some retirement money in a **tax-free Roth IRA**. While you'll contribute after-tax income, your withdrawals will be completely free of federal income tax provided your account has been open at least five years and you're at least 59½. Similar tax savings are available for college savings with a Coverdell education savings account (ESA) or a 529 college savings plan.

INVESTMENT PLANNING

Investment decisions have tax consequences, although minimizing taxes should be only part of your overall investment strategy. The investment risk you're willing to take, the return you can reasonably expect, and the impact of the transaction on your portfolio

DOING WELL BY DOING GOOD

You are entitled to deduct gifts you make to qualified charitable, religious, and educational organizations. The way you make the gift can have tax consequences. For example, you're likely to save on taxes by giving assets you own directly to the organization you want to benefit rather than selling the assets and making a cash gift.

The tax consequences of bequests you make to individuals, such as those to children and grandchildren, can be reduced as well by making those gifts in certain ways. Among the examples are creating trusts and avoiding the generation-skipping tax. Working with experienced legal and tax advisers as you make your plans is always wise and sometimes essential.

diversification are all at least as important as the tax implications.

Here's what you need to know:

- A **capital gain** is money you realize for selling an investment for more than you paid to buy it. A **capital loss** occurs when you sell an investment for less than it cost you.
- If you've owned an investment for more than a year before you sell, you have a **long-term capital gain or loss**. If it's been less than a year, you have a **short-term capital gain or loss**.
- Long-term gains are taxed at a lower rate than your ordinary income, while short-term gains are taxed as ordinary income. The long-term rate is determined by your adjusted gross income (AGI), and may be 0%, 15%, or 20%. Surcharges may apply, again depending on your AGI.
- You can use long-term capital losses to offset long-term capital gains, or short-term losses to offset short-term gains, on a dollar-for-dollar basis. Unused losses can be carried over from one tax year to the next.

So, as you make investment decisions, you may want to postpone sales when feasible to qualify for the long-term gain rate and sell some assets with capital losses at the end of the tax year to offset some gains.

USING PRETAX DOLLARS

If your employer offers a **flexible spending account (FSA)** as an optional employee benefit, it's a tax-saving opportunity you probably don't want to pass up. An FSA lets you set aside pretax income to pay for uncovered healthcare expenses, including copays, deductibles, prescription drugs, and many over-the-counter medications that meet the IRS standards for treating or preventing disease or illness.

An FSA usually works on a calendar year. To participate you contribute, through payroll deductions, as much as you think you'll spend during the year, up to the maximum of $2,500. If you and your spouse are both eligible to participate, each of you can contribute up the $2,500 limit.

There is one risk: If you don't use the money during the year for eligible expenses you may forfeit it. However, employers may offer either a two-and-a-half month grace period into the following year or allow you to access up to $500 of any unspent money in that year, removing some of the pressure of using up your balance.

Using an FSA does involve substantial paperwork, but it can provide real tax savings. For example, suppose you contributed the full $2,500 and spent it all on covered expenses. If you were in the 33% tax bracket, you would effectively have saved $825. In the 25% bracket, the saving would be $625. If you want more information, check IRS Publication 502, *"Medical and Dental Expenses."*

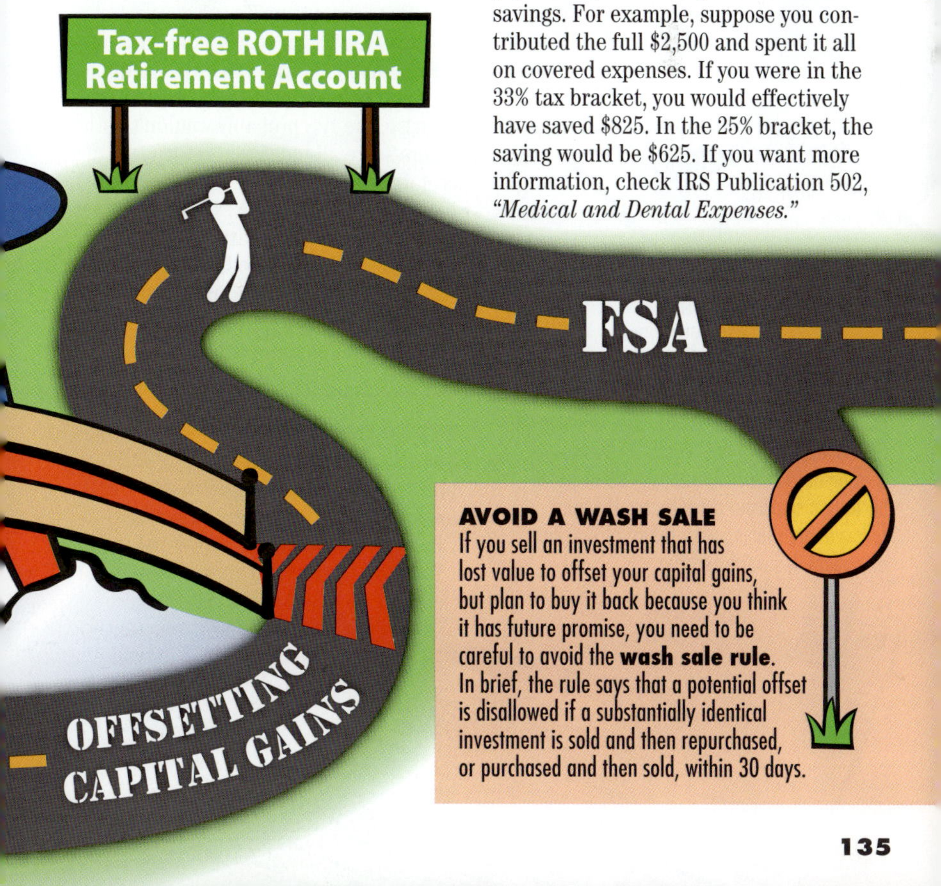

AVOID A WASH SALE

If you sell an investment that has lost value to offset your capital gains, but plan to buy it back because you think it has future promise, you need to be careful to avoid the **wash sale rule**. In brief, the rule says that a potential offset is disallowed if a substantially identical investment is sold and then repurchased, or purchased and then sold, within 30 days.

Keeping Records

To report what you owe and defend against a possible audit, you need a year's worth of records.

Just after the start of the new year, you'll begin receiving a host of tax documents. These include official third-party notifications, such as a W-2 that reports your salary or wages and a full range of 1099 forms that show your investment, retirement, and miscellaneous income. You may also receive a 1099-Q that reports tuition payments, and Schedule K-1s or Form 1065s that report partnership gains or losses.

The IRS expects you to report the information shown on these documents, which it matches to copies of its own. In addition, you must keep your own records of earnings from other sources, such as rental income, freelance work for which you don't receive a 1099, or royalties.

Similarly, you must have back-up for your expenses if you plan to itemize deductions or claim adjustments or credits.

Expense records should include the person or organization that was paid, date, type of expense, and business purpose. Regular entries in an electronic or paper expense log are a valid record in most cases, thought there are special record-keeping requirements for tips, business use of a car, travel and entertainment, and non-cash charitable contributions. You'll also need receipts for expenditures over $75 if the IRS asks for them.

There are individual IRS publications dealing with most recordkeeping topics, which you can find using the Search button on the IRS website.

WHAT'S AN AUDIT?

An audit is an IRS examination of your tax return and supporting records to determine if you've reported your situation correctly. The agency's going-in position combines a strong suspicion that you owe additional tax with the belief it will recapture substantial revenue. Otherwise, the IRS probably wouldn't bother.

IRS computers score all individual returns using a complex, secret discrimination index function (DIF) formula developed by its National Research Program to identify returns that are candidates for audit. There's also an Unreported Income DIF to identify returns that are likely to be concealing income. Both formulas are based on specific criteria that have been weighted for the probability of error or evasion.

A TAXPAYER'S BILL OF RIGHTS

IRS Publication 1, *"Your Rights As A Taxpayer,"* is often described as a taxpayer bill of rights because it spells out the rules the IRS must follow in questioning your return or handling an appeal. It's worth reading.

TYPES OF AUDITS

The IRS conducts three types of audits, plus what it calls an **adjustment**. With an adjustment, you receive a notice—CP-2000—that you owe additional tax.

You have the right to appeal, which you must do in writing within 60 days.

If you agree, however reluctantly, that the IRS is right, all you have to do is write a check.

HOW LONG SHOULD YOU KEEP YOUR RECORDS?

The IRS usually has three years—called a **period of limitations**—to audit your return, so you should keep all the relevant records at least that long. But it's important to keep some records longer.

If you've underreported your income by 25% or more, the IRS has six years to audit your return. And if you don't file, or you file a false return, they have forever.

Type of record	How long to keep it
Most records of income and expense	At least three years, seven if possible
Investment other than real estate	Until three years after you sell
Real estate (initial cost, improvements, costs of selling)	Until seven years after you sell
Tax returns	At least six years, ideally forever

WHO IS AT RISK?

In reality, only about 1% of all tax returns filed in any year are audited, though some groups of people are audited at a higher rate. The IRS focuses on high-income individuals, those with pass-through income from partnerships and S corporations, non-citizens with significant US earnings, and anybody who tries to claim there's no legal requirement to pay taxes.

Factors that may trigger an audit include:

- **Deductions that appear to be too large for your income**
- **Income and expenses for which there is no third-party reporting**
- **An unusually large tax refund**
- **Real estate rental losses**
- **Overseas bank accounts**

In the past, home office deductions were often questioned. But beginning with returns filed in 2014 there's a simplified method for claiming the deduction. If you follow these guidelines, you're much less likely to raise an IRS eyebrow.

SEND NO ORIGINALS

If you're providing backup documentation of your expenses or deductions, never send your originals to the IRS. Instead send photocopies. They could get lost and aren't ever returned. Either could pose a real problem if you need the information in the future.

THE APPEALS PROCESS

You have the right to ask for a review of any audit findings with which you don't agree. You appeal first to the examiner's supervisor and then to the IRS Appeals Office. IRS Publication 5, *"Appeal Rights and How to Prepare a Protest if You Don't Agree,"* outlines the process. You can represent yourself, though it may be wiser to use a qualified tax professional to handle the appeal.

As a last resort, you can take your case to court, though most litigation is expensive and slow. Depending on the size of the claim and whether you have paid the disputed amount, the case is heard in tax court, a federal district court, or federal claims court. The court of last resort is the US Supreme Court.

A **correspondence audit** is done by mail. The IRS asks you to send specific records to back up your return. If the documents support your entries, the matter may be resolved in your favor. But you may well owe additional tax.

An **office audit** is held in an IRS office with a tax auditor. You are told which areas of your return will be examined and what materials to bring with you.

A **field audit** is conducted by an IRS revenue agent in your home, office, or tax professional's office if that person is entitled to practice before the IRS. Your entire return and all supporting documents are subject to examination.

A

B

C

D

E

L

M

N

O

P

R

S